# The Magic of Meditation

## by
## Gordon Banta

The Mandala Press

distributed by

SUN RISING BOOKS

First Printing...2005

## THE MANDALA PRESS
## WWW.MANDALA-PRESS.COM

Publisher-Donette Smock
Editor-in-Chief-Dale Jungk
Cover Design-Donette Smock
Composite Editor–Anne-Marie Benson

Copyright © 2005 by **Gordon Banta**
ISBN: 1-933242-17-5

mandala press books
are distributed by

SUN RISING BOOKS
724 Felix
St. Joseph, Missouri 64501
U.S.A.
www.sun-rising-books.com
*Printed in the United States of America*

## DEDICATION

A special dedication to the love of my life, Lisa Clark.

# THE MAGIC OF MEDITATION

# CONTENTS

Introduction     07

| | | |
|---|---|---|
| Part One | HOW TO TUNE INTO THE SPIRIT | 19 |
| Chapter 1 | The Quest of the Spirit | 20 |
| Chapter 2 | The Quest of the Universal Spirit | 33 |
| Part Two | HOW TO TUNE INTO FLOWERS | 61 |
| Chapter 3 | The Quest of the Soul | 62 |
| Chapter 4 | The Quest of the Higher Self | 107 |

About the Author     136

# INTRODUCTION

This is the beginning of a new way of writing for me. I finally finished something I started over ten years ago.

I am now in the process of turning on my mind. What exactly do I mean when I say I am turning on my mind? I believe there are two ways of thinking: one way is to think creatively or intuitively. This I call instinctive thinking. Our logical mind, which I call the body mind, thinks through our electric senses. Our intuitive mind, which I call the spirit mind, thinks through the electromagnetic energy field called the soul, or our subconscious. This is our higher consciousness, our gateway to the higher self.

When we awaken after being asleep, our body comes alive again. Our senses become active and our body mind is activated, while our intuitive or spirit mind never sleeps. It is always active. We are not always aware of this because our body mind is the dominant side of our thinking when we are awake. We are aware of our intuitive mind only partially when we are awake or asleep.

Your mind is a single entity, but in order to understand this oneness of mind, you must divide it in two. Think about electricity. To understand electricity, you must also divide it in two. One side of the pole is male and the other is female; in other words, positive and negative, or electrical and magnetic.

Your mind works exactly the same way; in the left hemisphere of your brain, you have the male-positive, electrical, aggressive force. In the right hemisphere, you have the female-negative, which is receptive, magnetic, and intuitive. Let's explore each side a little more in depth.

The left side of the brain is the seat of your conscious mind. It is masculine in nature and projects thoughts out of your head, like a radio transmitter. Your subconscious mind, on the right side of your brain, receives thoughts like a radio receiver. Your body mind, or conscious mind, projects thoughts out of your head from the time you wake until the time you return to sleep. Your conscious (body) mind is only functioning when you are awake. It memorizes and records all day long. It projects these memories out of your head constantly in the form of electrical thoughts. It has no power to think, yet it seemingly thinks all day. From now on I will call the conscious mind the body mind, and the sub-conscious mind the spirit mind.

Your body mind cannot think up a single new thought. It can only project a thought it has memorized in the course of its development. It can never conceive of a new thought. It can, however, analyze or add to a thought or idea.

For example, Edison conceived of the light bulb through his spirit mind. You can add to or make better this light bulb through analyzing what you have memorized about electricity in school. If you haven't learned anything about it, you cannot add to it. You can add to the light bulb, however, by way of your spirit mind, because your spirit mind receives new thoughts in the form of ideas. In short, your body mind sends out electric thoughts while your spirit mind receives magnetic or creative thoughts.

## Left Hemisphere

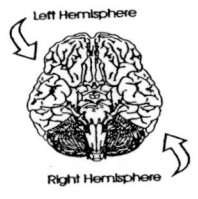

The two make one. Both sides of the brain are needed. The right side creates, while the left side manifests. Before anything appears in this physical universe, it first must be created in the ethers, or within the mind. Then the conscious mind proceeds to logically make it appear in the physical.

When a person makes a statement that he is psychic or intuitive, he or she is merely using the right brain, or the spirit mind. The same holds true with people who are artistic or inventive. But people who claim to be intelligent or all wise may not be using the right brain. I have met many people who appear to be extremely intelligent. But all they may have is a storehouse of memories. They deal with logic and a multitude of words, but they may not have real understanding. To know something instinctively is to know it. To know something intelligently is to accept it. When you know something instinctively, you know it from within. When you know something intelligently, you know it from the outside of your self. When you know something instinctively, you just know it; you do not always know how you know, you just know. Knowing something instinctively means that you know it psychically. It is like reading a book. You can read a book from cover to cover and memorize it completely, but you will only know the essence of the book. Let me give you an example.

If I tell you to read a book and give me the truth out of the book, you may give me back a very small portion of the book. If I ask you to tell me what you remember of the book, it may be a large portion of the book, yet only a small amount of it will still be true. Think about this paragraph very carefully. You will soon begin to know what I am saying. If you let the words become pictures, you will know what I am teaching you. Be alert, be aware, and let what I am giving you flow into your consciousness. If I discuss a particular subject in a book, I may be able to discuss it at great length, but that doesn't mean I know the book. I may only know a small portion of the book. Have you ever had a book and remembered every word you read? Did you know exactly what the book was teaching you? Or did you retain only the essence of the book? This essence comes to you by way of your subconscious mind.

People ask how I use the right side of the brain without the left interfering, since the left is always chattering like an endless sea of thoughts. Many teachers will tell you to be quiet to still the mind. They are referring to the conscious mind, or the left side. Some even refer to the left side as the ego. In any case, the best way to use the right side of your brain is to learn how to distinguish conscious thoughts from subconscious ones.

A conscious thought is something you have already known before. A subconscious thought is always something new, like an idea. For example: think of a dream you have had.

As soon as you wake up, you immediately start to forget the dream. Why? Because when you awaken, your senses have become activated.

Your senses are electrical; therefore, your body mind, which is connected to your senses, also becomes activated. You start thinking of your dream with your body mind. Your dreams always come from your spirit mind, so the more you think about the dream with the conscious, the more you forget it because the conscious wasn't there.

The conscious mind always wants to be in charge because it is aggressive and masculine in nature. The subconscious is always passive. However, it is truly the power side of your mind and always knows. The conscious always assumes. Whenever you assume something, you are sure to get yourself into trouble.

The body mind cannot think of two things at once, while the spirit mind can do anything conceivable. All dreams, new ideas, and all imagination are of the right side. All of your will comes from the left. The best way to tap into the right side is to relax your senses through meditation, self-hypnosis, relaxation therapy, etc. They are all one and the same anyway. Learn to daydream. Then learn to daydream constructively. While daydreaming, new thoughts and ideas will come to you, learn to trust them. They are real.

All thoughts that come to you come via the right side of your brain, the spirit mind.

These thoughts are real, and if you pay attention to them, you will find they can solve any problem, any difficult situation you might encounter and will truly help you in any and all ways. It is truly the power within often spoken about by wise people. Once again, I must repeat to you. Intuitive data is perceived through the right hemisphere of the brain while sensory and motor coordination is processed through the left hemisphere. The left side has to do with the reasoning and rationalizing part of your thinking, while the right side has to do with premonitions, hunches, art, creativity, and just plain old "gut" feelings.

Think of this. When you are absolutely stumped about a problem, when you can't get an answer, what do you do? You get up and walk away from it and the answer suddenly comes to you. You allow the answer to shift from the left side to the right side of the brain.

Traditionally, in our school systems, you are taught to read books and memorize them. You are only taught to use mechanistic forms of learning. If you were allowed to take time and intuitively perceive what you have read, you would have real understanding of the printed materials. You would then allow the information to sink deep into your subconscious mind, and that is where you truly start to learn. You can use this form of learning with everything and all forms of knowledge. I am going to show you how to use your right brain in what is known as the "field of psychic phenomenon."

Before reading each chapter, pause and take seven deep breaths. This will enable you to relax and you will be able to absorb more easily what I have written.

## Universal Mirror is called the

## Universal One or GOD.

The Universal Mirror is an action of which there has to be an equal and opposite reaction. The Universal Mirror is pure energy, a two-fold light wave of energy. What goes out from you is always reflected back to you. If you cause something to happen, it will be reflected back to you equally.

If you meditate on this Universal Mirror, it will reflect back to you anything that you desire. All inventions are created in this fashion.

This system works in opposite directions. If you take something, something will be taken from you. If you give something, something will be given back to you.

Whatever you see in another person, you are, in reality, seeing what is inside of yourself (Universal Mirror).

Whatever it is you do not like about someone, it is because you are seeing something in that person that is in you.

You cannot recognize in me anything that is not already in you. You can only recognize in me what is in you, mirrored back).

We live in a universe of mirrors. Until you recognize this fact, you will not understand life or the cause of it.

Any invention is only a reflection. It must be already in the Universal Consciousness and is, therefore, being reflected back to us. Everything that happens to you is happening because of this reflection. Your last life is being reflected back to you in this life and this life will reflect back to you when you reincarnate. Each time you read this, you will have a new and better understanding.

All created things are reflections from the Universal Mirror. Just as in this book.

Meditation:

Meditation is the art of listening.

Meditation is going within, so that something can be reflected back out.

Meditation is losing all awareness of the physical self so that the real self comes forward (Higher Self).

Meditation, therefore, is a tool towards reaching the Higher Self.

Meditation is a tool in developing Psychometry.

Meditation is an education, an education of the mind.

## Psychometry:

Psychometry is a tool towards self-knowledge.

Psychometry is the art of tuning in.

Psychometry is a reflection of the Universal Mirror.

Psychometry is soul reflection.

Psychometry is the truth.

Psychometry can be a form of meditation.

Psychometry is an aspect of meditation.
Psycho- means soul. Metry - is a measurement.
Psycho-metry.

# Part One:

# HOW TO TUNE INTO THE SPIRIT

# Chapter 1

# The Quest of the Spirit

I guess we have to start somewhere in our search for vision, which has been sought for eons before recorded time. It is the search for knowledge, the search for understanding. We demand enlightenment and the answer to the eternal question: to know...what?

To know about life and happiness. For what it is we are all seeking? Is it to understand oneself? To know who we are, or what we are, where we are going and why we are here?

Did you ever ask yourself, "Why is it everyone appears to be unhappy? Why can't we get along? Why is there always dissension? Why is it that today we can be absolutely happy, nothing can bother us, everything goes right and nothing is wrong and then tomorrow everything is the opposite?

Did you ever ponder these questions? If you did come up with an answer, you probably have changed it again and again, or you probably reasoned or rationalized through some answers until you came up with a solution that felt logical to you. Then, a few days later, you threw away those beliefs because you had outgrown them.

When I sat down one day to meditate, it came to me how people are dissatisfied and disgruntled with life. It seems that most people, especially those in Western society, do not get into the flow of the universe. Instead, they are in discord with the rhythm of the universe.

Quite often I am asked this question, "How, in fact, do we get into the ebb and flow?" My explanation goes something like this. Everything in the universe has a rhythm to it. If you know how to find this rhythm, you can begin to become happy and bring abundance into your life. One of the ways to find this rhythm is to become aware that everything you see and feel is alive. Everything pulsates with life. This entire planet that we live on is alive. Even the chair you sit on is alive. Believe me. If you open your inner sight, you will see for yourself that everything pulsates with life.

This life is sometimes called by other names, such as energy, electricity, or as the Chinese say, "Chi."

I call it an electro-magnetic energy field or the aura. Everything has an aura or soul. When scientists talk about the ozone, they, in fact, are talking about the aura, or soul of this planet. I will explain this in my book about auras.

Native Americans teach that there is an exact location somewhere on this planet that will create the feeling of well-being, a homey feeling, a comfortable spot where you can go to be in harmony with the elements.

There is an exact spot for everyone. If you are having a difficult time, a real struggle, you just may be living in the wrong location. Some people migrate to other parts of the country, or world, and all of a sudden everything goes right for them. This is because they landed in the right energy field for them. You can do the same. Go to a good psychic and ask if you are living in the right location, and then take a trip to the place that he or she recommends. Just go for a vacation and see if your psychic is right. You will "feel"' it. All you have to do is be sensitive about that area and you will definitely feel it. When I go to Colorado, I feel it instantly. I feel like I am home.

Try this. Whenever you go into a room, close your eyes and sense where the best or most comfortable location in the room is for you. You don't have to try this only in a room. You can try it anywhere. Think about it, and then try it when you enter an airplane, aboard a ship, or just walking in a forest. If you practice this method, you will slowly start to get in tune with yourself, your Higher Self that is. You will start to get in tune with people, animals, and especially inanimate objects.

Not only is there a proper place for you on this planet, but there is a proper time for you as well. There is a time to do any and all things. A sense of timing is in everything. Timing, perhaps, is everything in this physical manifestation anyway. In the Spirit World there is no thing as time. You just are. Or you just exist.

There are twelve months in a year and each month has a position in time and space. This also applies to each day, hour, minute, and second. These positions are extremely important to you in your daily life. To be at the right position at the exact time can be rewarding or disastrous for you. I was on a radio show with Shirley McLaine once, and she told me that the word "disaster" means to disassociate you from the astral plane. It made sense. To be in a disastrous situation means to become disassociated from the truth, to be out of balance, to miss the mark.

If you tune into this interrelationship between time, space and energy, you can find the key to your success and happiness in life. You may learn the secrets of the universe.

Want another clue? Just look back upon your own life. Was there a time when you had peace, balance, and prosperity? Did you have the right friends and relatives? Are you firmly rooted into your lifestyle today? Are you firmly rooted into your home, your town, or state? Is it right for you? If not, then move and do it now. If it is right then seek to make it better.

Allow your intuition to tell you if you attract the right people, the right home, or the right work. In short, start using your right brain, your spirit mind, which is your true mind and the best friend you have. Your spirit mind will always lead you in the right direction for it is directly linked to your higher self your true self.

Sometime when you are all alone and there is a thunderstorm coming your way, mentally picture the sun shining right where you are sitting (you must be outside, of course). Then go about the business of thinking about everything else except the rain. Block the rain out of your head and let the image that you have pictured in your mind to flow to the back of your mind. Soon you will notice that the storm has either changed direction or the clouds have split and it will rain all around you, but not on you. Be sure to try this when you are alone, because another person's disbelief will alter the effects of your projections. It is very easy and very simple to perform this experiment, yet it can become very difficult by the very fact of one's disbelief.

Once mastered, never do this at random or just for fun. Why upset the balance of nature? Just do it when it is really important. Lone Wolf, of the Kiowa tribe, once made a famous speech to Ulysses S. Grant, then President of the U.S. In part of his speech he said, "For I am the one who can make it rain and I am the one who can make it not rain."

You can make it rain just as easy as you can make it not rain. I found that when you do, you could cause flooding. Be extremely cautious when you are playing with Mother Nature. You are playing with magic. This is the mark of a true magician. And we are all magicians. If not, then we are all mindless.

Always remember you are living in a universe that is alive. There is no such thing as death. Nothing dies. Everything lives. Even at the point we call death, your body does not die, it simply decomposes. It changes, but the atoms and molecules that make up your physical body does not die. They only change and go somewhere else and become a part of something else. They just go back to where they came from, Mother Earth. Then they become seeds for new life everywhere. Whenever you look into a mirror, remember, that body is not you. It is a creation of you. And each and every day, it is being created and de-created.

Life goes on and on. We can become aware of this, if we try, or should I say, if we let it. It is an art to learn to live in harmony with the land. You have to become like an artist. You have to paint the harmony in your mind first. Then allow it to manifest itself in your daily actions. Watch the birds or other animals. Watch the trees or clouds. They will always give you a true picture of what is actually going on.

The clouds will always give you a clue. They will form a picture perhaps of a person, scene of a lake, or mountain. Watch carefully and they will always show you something. When I say, "watch," I mean, "look in a special way." Allow your eyes to go soft the way you do when you are daydreaming. Allow the tree to go out of focus, or the cloud, whichever you are watching.

Can you remember when you've been watching a fire how it hypnotizes you? (Or should I say, "mesmerizes" you?) Remember while looking into a fire how you could actually see images of shapes, people, animals, images of almost anything? Well, this is the flame showing a message. All you have to do is learn what the symbol of the image means and you will know what the fire is telling you.

I know that if you get relaxed enough to see an image in a fire or tree, you are also relaxed enough to wait for the tree or flame to give you the meaning of the image. This is what I mean by "telling you." Just be patient and wait. The answer will come to you soon.

I remember meeting an astrologer once who told me that he intuitively sees symbols in a chart. Then he knows the whole picture of the chart that he is reading. He then takes his time and, like a puzzle, he slowly puts the pieces together. You see, each symbol for him is like an image. He then lets the chart tell him what it means rather than letting his intellect tell him from the masses of information he has stored in his head from memory.

Astrology is like anything else. You can learn it by storing masses of information in your head and then reciting it from memory, or you can learn it intuitively and know what you need to know when you are reading a chart. Actually, very little information is needed if you learn how to use your intuition, which is what this book is all about.

Let me explain it a little further. The astrologer has studied astrology charts for year. Each symbol in the chart has a special meaning for him. However, each person for whom he is reading is unique. There will never be another person like the one receiving the reading. So how could the symbols always be true? They can't. So he does the next best thing. He lets the symbols become images in his mind (imagination) and then lets the images tell him what they mean. There will always be similarities but never the exact same reading. Allow this information I am giving you to just flow into your inner mind, your spirit mind.

Come back to it later and you will understand my meaning. You have to sense what I am saying here and not to think about it logically.

When people go into the forest or a cave to have a vision, the vision will most certainly come. Yet, will they be able to interpret it? Most students will go back to their teacher, which is the best way to find out what their vision meant. However, I believe you do not have to do this. You can teach yourself to know your dreams and visions.

I have had visions all of my life, but I did not recognize them. I thought I was just daydreaming. They did not mean anything to me until I went to classes. In a class of psychic development, I learned many things. Some of those things I already knew, but now I know them better because the teacher put new meaning and new words to it.

Then I realized that things sometimes come in flashes. Sometimes they come as symbols, but until you can know what symbols are or what they mean, you do not even know that you have had a vision. Visions come sometimes as ideas; they are clothed with many different meanings. In an upcoming book, I will explain symbols in detail. The difference between a good psychic and a not-so-good one is determined by if he or she can read symbols.

A card reader is merely reading symbols; the symbol points the reader in a certain direction. It leads the card reader to know what to look for psychically. You can read a person hundreds of different ways, because the main part of reading someone lies within the symbols of the signs that you get along the way.

Symbols are the basis of all psychic intuitions. They may come in all forms: numbers, colors, dreams, ideas, and words.

If someone asks me a question, first I must determine if the person is asking me a psychic question or just a question he or she is asking me intelligently or a question from the heart or the head. Then I will either tune into the question or just merely receive whatever answer I may

have.  Most people think that I am always going to give them the right answer and when I don't, they think I was "off" that day intuitively.
 Actually all I did was to give them the answer the same way everyone else does off the top of the head.  But if I tune into the question, then I have a 90 percent chance of giving them the right answer.

Let me put it to you this way.  If someone asks me an ordinary question, I will go to my conscious (body) mind and give information that is stored in my memory bank, ordinary answers.  But if I am asked a more important question, and it must be stated to me this way, then I will go to my (spirit) mind and give them the answer.

I intend to teach you how to do this.  Before we can begin, we must talk about philosophy and enlightenment.  I believe that philosophy usually dies with the philosopher, unless the philosopher is enlightened.  Then his philosophy inspires people to grow more, to become more aware and to add to that philosophy.  The philosophy changes; it does not remain the same.  The philosophy becomes outdated.  We no longer need it, yet was the philosophy wrong?

Let me give you an example: When you were in the eighth grade you had the philosophy of an eighth grader. When you were in the 12th grade, you had the philosophy of a 12th grader. You may have laughed at a 12th grader's philosophy when you were in the eighth grade, but you needed the one to get to the other. A 12th grader won't laugh at an eighth grader's philosophy. He or she would just think, "Oh well, he is getting there."

So, we too, are always growing, always learning something in spite of ourselves. Why do we have to make an effort to learn? Why do we do the things we do? Why is it one evil act can make a person's life miserable, a life which otherwise might have been happy, content and productive? Because we cannot know everything about the visible universe because it is endless. However, we can know the invisible and the Universal Spirit is invisible. So, let's get in tune with this Spirit. It is the only way we can know anything. So now is the time to learn to know a little about the Universal Spirit.

BREATHE...
BREATHE...
BREATHE...

# Chapter 2

# The Quest of the Universal Spirit

Meditation is the art of listening. Man has learned how to pray, yet he has rarely learned how to listen. Listening is meditation, or contemplation, going within. Praying is sending outward. Praying is projection out of you. You ask God to listen to you.

Meditating is an effort to listen to God. When you pray, you must also meditate for the prayer to be effective. If you ask me a question, you pause, you hesitate, and you wait for the answer. You listen. Most people, when they pray, don't wait for the answer. They do not pause and listen. Usually they panic if it's a life or death situation or they might immediately go off in different directions. The main reason for this is that we don't know how to listen. We don't really believe that God is listening to our prayers or we wouldn't keep asking for the same thing over and over. If we really believed our prayer would be answered, we would only need to ask but once. Then we would say over

and over "Thank you, thank you." By saying thanks, we believe that it is actually going to happen.
The prayer would be answered when it was time to be answered, just as Mother Nature works in her own due time with everything in its own season and not when we think it should be answered.

When beginning to meditate, you must sit, relax, and wait and listen. Second, you must know how to listen. The Universal Mind, God, is constantly talking to us, but we are too busy to take the time to pause to meditate daily and to listen. The Universal One is perpetually bombarding us with thoughts, ideas, feelings, and visions. When an idea or a thought comes into your head, it has to come from somewhere.

Our minds are projecting thoughts constantly, something like 10,000 per day. Some say much more. Our minds are thinking about these thoughts and perhaps even analyzing them. So you see, mediation is the art of listening between these thoughts.

When someone is speaking, listen to what is being said. Then listen to what is not being said.

Now you will know what the person is really saying. You will have the true picture.

In the same way when you are reading, read between the lines and let the sense of what is being said flow into your mind. This is true thinking. Many people see only what is going on in the universe. They only use half of their mind.

Meditation will teach you to use the other half. Then you will become aware of what true thinking is. At this very moment our thoughts flow so continuously that there appears to be no space between them. If you concentrate upon the moment, when one thought disturbance has entered your mind and another thought has not yet started, then and there you will be in that relaxed state known as meditation.

If you can force your attention between these same two thoughts, you will be seeing behind the mind, for the mind is nothing but a continuous flow of thought pattern. If you can see between two successive thoughts, you must and will be face to face with the symbols. Once you focus your attention between the thoughts, there will be no thoughts. You will be in tune with the Infinite. This will be pure cosmic awareness, awareness that alone is in all thought.

Thought is nothing more than being conscious of an object. For this to happen, your mind must be calm and still. This is what is known as pure happiness, or bliss, the serenity of being.

We must try to define the mind, for we cannot know thoughts simply because we are trying to understand them with the mind. Without thought, there is no mind. The mind is the flow of thoughts, as the river is the flow of water. Your whole purpose in life is to reach as high as you possibly can with your creative mind, to be as in tune with your higher self, as you can be. To reach the highest unfolding you can possibly reach is to know who you are and to know the Universal Mind.

Of course, the highest level of consciousness is to be illuminated into the Light of Knowing, also known as Cosmic Consciousness. If you could but receive one small spark of that light, you would possess the greatest thing you could ever possibly achieve. The purpose of this book is to help you to achieve another step in that direction. Then you can become aware of your pure divine-self.

That divine spark of light lies within everyone just waiting to illuminate the soul. Your soul has been seeking this light of oneness since the beginning of time. Allow me to point you into that direction, and of course by helping you, I am also helping myself.

As long as you have been incarnated into your electrically sensed body, you have always been seeking pleasure. Pleasure is of the senses and is short-lived, while happiness is of the spirit and lasts forever. As long as the light of knowing lies dormant within you, you can only know pleasure. You may have small glimpses of happiness, but you may not recognize it as such. As long as this light lies dormant within you, you can only be aware of your mortal body, which lives and dies many times. You will think that your body is yourself.

When that spark of light is awakened within, you will have extraordinary knowledge and exceptional powers. As soon as this light is awakened within you, you will become known as a genius. There are many levels of consciousness. The first is in the mineral

kingdom; second is plant; third is animal; and fourth is barbaric man, which is where most people are today.
Genius, which is the beginning of unfolding back into the Light of God is fifth; Cosmic Consciousness is sixth; and seventh, Christ Consciousness.

Man in his barbaric stage thinks that he is his body, that everything outside of him is what counts. He thinks through his electrically sensed body. He thinks, hears, and sees outwardly through his eyes and ears and the rest of his senses.

The genius that lies inward, and then manifests the creations outwardly through his or her senses is how every true inventor, painter, sculptor, writer or composer works. The genius can hear sounds in all of nature, such as listening to the trees, flowers, etc. They can see with their inner eyes the forms and patterns of light that are already existent all around us.

Light is the answer to all things. If you listen to the inner sounds, it is the most beautiful sound, and if you see the light patterns and shapes, it is a rhythm that will make your heart sing. If you can raise your level of consciousness to genius, you will become a co-creator with the Universal Consciousness, the universal heartbeat that lies within us all.

The world of man has almost completely gone mad. Look around you, and you will see it, but if you look within, then you will see the beauty of it all. Man must think outwardly in order to exist in this physical universe. But if he becomes aware of his true nature, his inward thinking will influence his outward thinking and he will be able to create a beautiful life.

Society is male dominated, and that is why we have wars, rape, murder, and madness. We must bring the feminine principle into our thinking. Now I am not talking man versus woman. That is one of the problems of nature. What I am referring to here is the electrically sensed conscious mind versus the magnetically sensed subconscious mind. One is masculine, electrical, and forceful and deals with all things outside of him while the other is feminine, magnetic, passive, and creative and deals with all things within him.

If we could see into our past lives, we would see that we wore many masks, many different personalities, but each is a step toward that

God-awareness that lies within each and every one of us. No one is lost. No one will perish forever. We will all make it, but some may seem to have more agony in awaiting its journey. This journey is long for all of us. We must have many reincarnations before we can become aware of our true nature. Each life is leading us closer and closer. Each day and each shining new hour gets closer to our greatest goal. Many times I am asked, "What is my goal or destiny in this life?" And I tell them to help find out who and what we are, why we are here, and where we are going. This is the greatest thing to find out when you are on the path to enlightenment, and meditation is the best path. There are many paths. Some are harder than others and we are all on a path. It is just that some paths are easier than others. The best path for me is meditation.

No matter what your karma is, you can overcome it through meditation. Do not put limitations upon yourself. Whatever you see inside of your head, you will become. Envision only the highest. See yourself as Christ saw himself and you will rise as high as you can. He said, "The things that I do, you can do also."

When I was about three years old, I was walking across a bridge with my mother and twin brother. The bridge was a small one that went across a lake. I stubbed my toe and fell into the lake. I can remember it as though it happened yesterday. I remember moving my arms back and forth in a thrashing motion and I can remember drinking the water. I also remember it did not hurt to drink the water. Then all of a sudden, I was floating above the lake and I could see the people diving into the water. I watched them pull me out of the water, but before they did, I remember going into a tunnel of darkness. It was a good feeling. Then I saw the Light. It was brilliant and inviting. There were hundreds of people there calling my name. I knew them all. Then someone told me to go back. I remember spinning backwards and then feeling dizzy. This is when I came to and someone was pushing on my stomach. It was an incredible experience.

Two years later, my twin brother threw a rock up into the air. He did this a lot. Just before it would hit, he would yell, "Look out!" Well, this time he went up to the attic and bombed me. It hit me on top of the head. I remember hearing my mother screaming, and my grandfather picking me up. I was covered in blood. I watched him carry me to the phone where he called an ambulance. I remember sitting on top of the ambulance.

I can remember calling out to my mother and grandfather as they were sitting in the ambulance. I could not understand why they did not see me. I was crying because I could not get inside.

When we arrived at the hospital, I even remember sitting on top of the elevator. It was an old gate type, not enclosed. I was on top looking down at my mother, grandfather, and three other people.

Suddenly the elevator started to spin and I was in the black tunnel again. This time I did not want to go back. People were yelling at me to go back. I did not recognize any of them. When I approached the light, I could not enter it and once again I spiraled backwards into consciousness. Of course, all of this did not make sense to me at that age. I did not realize what had happened to me until I was thirty-five years old.

Meditation Explained:

Meditation is an exercise of the mind, the quieting, calming, and taming of the mind. Meditation is not a physical act. It has nothing to do with the environment, nor the posture in which one sits. The postures are only to allow relaxation.

Always have the proper attitude when entering into a relaxed state of mind. The best way to do this is to think of a spiritual being, or perhaps a calm place such as a forest or a beach. Allow your mind to drift off to such a place or to drift off to meet your guardian angels or spirit guides. Then begin a breathing exercise. I like to breathe in very deeply through the nostrils, filling up my lungs and stomach, at least seven, but never more than ten times. It can be very detrimental to your meditative state if you overdo breathing exercises.

I then focus my mind upon a place, such as a beach. I focus all of my attention upon the waves rolling in gently before me. I take notice of the deep blue sky and the pure white clouds. I become in tune with the gentle breezes blowing upon my face. I may even notice a beautiful hawk in my mind, or an eagle soaring high in the wind. I even allow this magnificent bird to draw my spirit up into his body and feel the energy of the wind carry me upward and onward into the meadows of my mind. Try practicing this method daily and soon you will be adding new scenes and be traveling into rainbows of color. You may even be joined by a spirit friend in these exercises. You simply can't imagine how beautiful your meditations will become. The most important part of meditation is in the breathing. I will go more into this later.

When meditating, you will notice all the pressures and stresses of the day leaving you. You will find yourself becoming happier and you will be able to handle life's tremors with great ease. The secret to life is to become calm and relaxed. Then life will be a treasure instead of a woe.

Before you begin to get involved in meditation, you should be aware of what the mind does. Meditation is a taming of the mind. We all have a mind. We all know that the mind is terribly agitated, worried, and anxious. It is often in tension, distress, and strain. How do we even know that the mind really exists? Ask yourself this question: What exactly is the mind?

The mind is pure and simple thought. This thought has power if it is envisioned. If you see what you think, the thoughts you think will become manifest. I am referring to seeing with your mind's eye, not your naked eye. Knowing this, you can command your body to be perfect. I do not or at least have not been ill for many years. I simply do not allow it. Sickness is not in my visions. You can command your life to be overflowing, to be happy, and to handle any task that may seem discomforting to you. Seeing makes it so. What you see is what you become. This is the only way to think. This is positive thinking. There is no other way to think positive. Some people write about positive thinking, yet they do not fully understand it. Seeing is believing. If you want to know what a person believes, do not listen to what he or she is saying, rather watch his actions. A person projects his beliefs in his actions. Action speaks louder than words.

True meditation is learning to commune with God. Once you learn to commune with God, you will then work knowingly and happily with him.

Meditation is thinking within your heart or your soul, rather than outwardly with your body or ego. Think of this. When you are in deep sleep, is there a mind? You may think not because you may lose all awareness of your mind, but the mind is always there, either attracting new thoughts or projecting old ones. If you want to meditate for a reason to grow spiritually or to heal yourself, you should visualize why you are doing this.

You must first put something into it. You cannot spend your whole life drawing out of a bank account unless you first put something back into it. You should always have the attitude that you are going to meditate for some good reason. If you need something, you must believe it will come to you. Visualize it very clearly and hold it in the back of your mind. You should not dwell on it. You must let it flow to the back of your mind. This way you retain the thought without dwelling on it.

When I first got into meditation, it took me three months before I began to leave my body to soul travel. The secret in meditation, I believe, is in the breathing. The second secret of meditation is to point your mind in a desired direction. When I first began to meditate, I desired to know about God. I also wanted to know who I was. So I pointed my meditation in a spiritual direction. I asked the Christ to come inside of me, to walk with me, and to talk to me. I only thought about him. I used music and breathing daily to get nearer to him. Within two months, I felt his presence.

About three months into it, I began to leave my body. It was a frightening experience at first. The first thing I noticed was that I could hear myself breathing, yet I knew that I was not breathing. I know this does not make sense, yet I kept saying to myself that I was not breathing. This is because I was out of my body and did not know it. At the first sign of fear, I crashed back into my body. I was trembling and did not meditate for about two or three weeks. Then I started meditating again.

I went to the state that I was in previously. I decided to not become frightened. I then heard a voice that said, "Open your eyes; open your eyes." So I opened my eyes only to notice that I was looking down on the back of someone's head. I soon noticed that his hair was curly and it appeared to be moving as if it were alive. I then realized that I was looking at my own head and became frightened and soon landed back into my body again. It took me another three months to get up nerve to proceed.

I knew that I should have had a teacher. If I had, I would have known what was happening. I know now that everyone should have a teacher. It is the only true way to go. I did have a teacher that taught me an awareness of my psychic abilities, but he did not teach me anything about meditation.

Remember, whatever you desire will come in many forms. It comes suddenly, but it surely will come. Whenever you meditate, always do it for a good reason. Allow yourself to give, and then allow yourself to receive. It seems like many people in this world do not know how to receive or accept a gift.

Whatever you give, it will always be given back to you. This holds true with everything in life. Meditation is really like having a conference with your higher self, for your higher self will lead you to the awareness of God, or to the Universal One. You can then learn to think your knowingness into material forms. You can manifest anything that you desire to the extent of your awareness of the Creator within you. Your spirit mind is your eternal being. Your body mind is a fleeting passing thing. It is short-lived. We are here in a whisper and gone in a whisper. Yet, our true nature is eternal. Your body mind records memories, experiences, and information electrically just like a tape recorder. The nerves of your body carries messages just like a telephone line. Your brain is the recorder and distributes the messages by way of the nervous system throughout your body. There is no power in the brain or in the nervous system. They only work through a command system, which is your spirit mind.

You will learn to think, to visualize forms into physical manifestations, and to give formed bodies into imagined thought forms. By following up your thought with actions, you will become a co-creator with God. Whatever your lot in life, whatever happens to you, is caused by you. If you are not happy, if you are having a run of bad luck, you have created this with your imagined thought forms, and probably unknowingly. You are your own creation. In your own meditation you will become aware of this. No one can harm you unless you give that person permission.

You must have seen the person hurting you deep within your subconscious mind (spirit-mind). But you were unaware of this happening to you. You can't control your body's actions through unbalanced thinking. By keeping your interchanges and interactions in absolute balance is to work knowingly with God. Put Him in all of your affairs and actions and you will succeed perfectly. Try it, first by meditating and then by daily actions. You are not perfect, at times you will slip, but persevere and you will succeed.

Your body becomes overwhelmed with toxins. These toxins are the direct result of fear, tension, stress, worrying, and other various emotions. You will be constantly bombarded with these toxins that destroy your body until you become aware that there is a higher force and that this force will work for your highest good. You must work with the Creator.

We co-create with Him when we relax into the silence and think thought-forms of ideas and then give these ideas formed bodies.

Your spirit mind is related to the invisible universe of cause, while your body is related to the visible universe of effect. The Creator's mind has one idea, which is creation as a whole. He has one desire to give creative expression to that idea. He creates His universe by thinking and imagining.

When I give readings, I tune into people's auras, which is their soul. While gazing at a person's soul, I will see thought forms coming out of his or her head. These thought forms appear as images. I can tell what is going on in a person's life just by gazing at the aura and talking about the images. If you can't see these images, then you can feel them. By feeling them, you can let them form pictures inside your head. A builder conceives the idea of a building inside of his or her head then puts it down on paper. Then the formed body of the building appears in the likeness of the builder's conception.

Whatever your desire, it will come in many forms. Clothe your thoughts or desires with all of the necessary materials that it will take and then proceed to manifest those same forms in your likeness with a material body.

Whenever you meditate, always do it for a good reason. Always have something worthwhile that you want to manifest in this material world and one that will benefit all. Meditation will help you open up your spirit mind. Some people will sit in a corner somewhere for the purpose of meditating. They will then try to stop their mind from thinking. If you think that isn't hard to do, sit down somewhere and try to stop your mind from projecting thoughts. They cannot be forced to stop.

Meditating is relaxing your physical body so that your (body) mind becomes void so that you will become aware of your spirit mind. Your spirit mind is quiet and receives thoughts flowing into your mind. Thoughts constantly flow into your mind, but all you have to do is direct whatever you want to flow into your mind. For instance, if you want to know about something, just ask your spirit for the answer and it will come to you. You just to have to be aware of how it will come. It will then flow into your head. It will come in the form of a thought that you did not know before. It may also come as an idea, or you may actually see something in your mind's eye. You may simply get a deep-down gut feeling inside. You must pay attention and you must believe the answer because your body mind will always, or nearly always, disagree with your answer. This is because your body mind is your logical mind and it only contends with the present. It always analyzes and operates strictly with logic.

You cannot know everything simply by reason, logic, or through analyzing it. If you relax your body mind, you will be able to receive thoughts or ideas. If you sit in meditation for 20 minutes today and get one new thought or idea, it is truly astounding. You will be excited, too. For instance, when I wanted to know something about a certain number in my numeroscope, I would first think about the number. Then I would proceed to meditate.

Once in a meditative state, however, the ideas and new thoughts about the number came pouring into my mind. Start now with these admonitions in your mind. Stretch out your hand and grasp the higher self of whom you have never perhaps made use, save in grave emergencies. Life can be an emergency most grave.

Your higher self is beside you so cleanse your brain and strengthen your will. It will take possession. It awaits you. Start tonight. Start now upon this new journey. Be always on your guard. Whichever entity controls you, the other hovers at your side. Beware lest the negative one enter, even for a moment.

Higher knowledge will come through the unfolding of intelligence within you (higher self) which leads you to discover the light (higher self) within, and which will ultimately lead you to oneness with God.

If you have an idea, it has to come to you from within, for an idea cannot be sensed by you, it can only be known. You cannot know anything unless you transcend your senses for your senses cannot know anything. They can but sense the effects of motion.

You cannot find love while in the taking stage of your evolution of which man is still in. He takes rather than gives. Taking breeds fear, greed, and imbalance. Love has not entered into man's life yet. Balance is the key word here. Look around you and you will see that most corporations and governments are still in the physical stage where its values are materialistic. Most people do not know what is wrong with civilization. This is because the higher self has not entered into the body or its daily affairs. Until this happens, we will live in an unbalanced world. Do not wait for your fellow man; you can help him more through right action. Allow the Father to enter into all of your affairs and the world will have a whole new outlook.

I will give you a step-by-step method in preparing your own personal meditation altar. An altar or shrine according to Webster's dictionary means "an object as an altar, temple or chapel or a spot or some considered sacred because of its relation to some holy person or miraculous event or because of its character and historical associations."

I believe that a shrine or altar is where you will meet your higher self and through that self meet the Universal One, (God). It is a place where you temporarily withdraw from the physical world and join with the Spiritual One. It is a place of communion and prayer, through meditation. It is a tranquil place, a place most secure where you can tap into the infinite resources of God. To some, an altar may be a place entirely within one's self and have no outer place, or it can be a special place within your home or office.

Remember that the altar is just a place to visit for spiritual reasons and meditation. It should be treated like a Holy place. It should be clean, not only physically but also spiritually and mentally clean as well. However, you do not even have to have an altar.

You can just go to the same place whether it be a favorite chair or corner of a room.
You do not even need to perform a daily ritual or ceremony, just a place that you can visit daily. If you sometimes find yourself too busy to have an exact time to meditate, then use the time that you have. I started out meditating three times a day. Now I am really busy and usually only meditate in the evening. Sometimes, however, I start the day off with meditation when I have the time.

I would like to help you set up your shrine and to do this, I would like you to use a small room, if possible. It is best if you have a small table as well. First, place two white candles on it. If Jesus is your spiritual leader, then place a picture of him on the table. If not Jesus, perhaps it is Buddha or some other Deity. It can be helpful if you also use other colored candles, such as blue, green, violet, or gold.

Color is important, yet it does not matter if you have an icon of a different color than I mentioned. I like to use quartz crystal and amethyst on my table. In fact, I have a lot of different stones that I have blessed. I also have a shaman's staff that I made myself. I make these staffs for my friends and students. I hand carve power animals on them, put feathers and crystals on them. Then I do a special ceremony to bless them so that they possess power.

I use cedar, sage, and sweet grass and smudge myself. Then, I offer tobacco to the Great White Spirit (White-Light). I offer the staffs up to the winged, the four-legged, two-legged, the creeping and the crawling, and the fish at sea. I then say "Ho-Mytokeweosi" which means "to all of my relatives." I learned this ceremony from Wallace Black Elk, a Lakota Spiritual Leader. And in my meditations with my Spirit Guide, Lone Wolf, Chief of the Kiowa, the shaman that can make it rain, and not rain, I send up smoke signals (messages or prayers) to "Tekunsila," the Great Spirit, for all of my friends. I have people that need healing and I send a smoke signal for them. It really works. Lone Wolf told me in meditation that this is the true way to send smoke signals. Not with a blanket high on a mountain top like they do in the movies. I have my eagle feathers and the feathers of the Great Horned Owl that I use to fan the smoke. When I do this ceremony, I create power. And if you ever want to feel power, come to my ceremonies.

So place a picture of someone that inspires you on your altar or hang it on the wall. Create a feeling of harmony in your room, with soothing colors and pictures. Or just use a small table and make it your personal shrine. Place energy there with your heart. Do everything in that room with your heart, never your head.

I sometimes use incense as well, but that should be up to you. Above all, you should have a picture of your Master teacher. I also use a crystal ball for it can truly aid you in your meditation. Everyone is different and has different tastes. All have different ideas about how to build a shrine. You can make it elaborate or simple or as I said you can just sit in a corner somewhere to meditate.

Now let me guide you into another method of meditation. Get a straight-back chair, sit straight up, spine erect, and don't let your back touch. Have both feet flat on the floor, your hands on your lap.

Bow your head slightly and place your tongue so that it slightly touches the top of your mouth. Imagine in your mind that you are a pump. As you slowly raise your head upwards, you will breathe in slowly and deeply. While breathing in, imagine that you are drawing a golden nectar from the base of your spine all the way up to the top of your head. Remember, do this slow and rhythmically. Slowly draw this nectar all the way up to the top of your head. Then without the slightest bit of hesitation, breathe out and imagine that this golden light, or nectar, is flowing down from the top of your head, down through the roof of your mouth, through your tongue and down into your throat, chest, and heart. When it flows into your heart, imagine your heart turning into a golden egg, and then imagine it flowing in your bloodstream and changing your blood from red to gold, like the nectar.

Now I know that you cannot visualize all of this at once. It may take you a few weeks, but if you work at it, you will discipline your mind and you will experience a rich and rewarding meditation. Practice this daily, even several times a day if you can. Remember never take more than ten deep breaths at a time, drawing in the golden nectar. I cannot tell you enough about not doing this, because it can be extremely dangerous. It is like the sun; sit in it a little while and it can heal you; sit in it for too long of a period and it will burn you.

I guarantee that if you practice this meditation with the higher self in mind, you will grow immensely. You will begin to have the most beautiful experiences.

I would like to refer back to the shrine at this point. I also have on my shrine Indian artifacts such as arrowheads, etc. I have a statue of a Mayan God as well. I do not pray to the Mayan gods, however. Anything that will aid you in focusing your attention upon something spiritual each day is what's important. Rededicate your shrine or holy place with the White Light. You will soon notice a difference there. If anyone visits your shrine, he or she will feel a tranquil presence there. Ask the Great Spirit to bless and touch each article on your shrine and bless the room itself before meditating, always visualize the White Light surrounding the room and you as well. Be relaxed, be calm, be still, and know.

Breathe...

Breathe...

Breathe...

# Part Two:

# HOW TO TUNE INTO FLOWERS

# Chapter 3

# The Quest of the Soul

Psychometry is basically two words, "psycho" meaning soul and "metry" meaning to measure- to measure the soul or spirit. A new depth of reality and experience will be discovered when inanimate objects are treated as personalities rather than as mere objects. Actually, there is no such thing as an inanimate object. Life is everywhere, in the trees, the clouds, and the earth. We have never learned to communicate silently with nature. The Native Americans have. I learned this from Wallace Black Elk as well. He was a great teacher. He never said he was teaching me anything. But I learned by observing. You can learn from everyone this way. So everyone can be a teacher. It is what you want to learn that is the question. I wanted to learn the Native American way, the Lakota way. That is one of the best ways of learning. They have a rich culture, and a beautiful one at that.

The psychometric sense is one of the senses that everyone possesses. Our minds are like radios. We project thoughts all day and simultaneously we receive thoughts. We keep receiving thoughts all through the night when we are sleeping. We are not always aware of it, but it is that simple. I can tame my mind and receive all night long if I so desire to and you can too. We are almost never aware of the messages we receive; we are only aware of the messages we transmit. We need to learn to strike a balance. Psychometry is an excellent way of learning to do just that. When your mind is balanced, you will receive as many thoughts as you are sending. This is the creative way of thinking.

Before we get involved in psychometry, I would like to point out something. If you have the idea that psychometry is evil or of the occult or it is way over your head, please dismiss these notions. It is far from being over your head. Psychometry, right now, is in your head and in your soul, your heart, and your spirit. It is in all of your physical, emotional, and mental makeup.

It is entirely possible for you to become attuned to the vibrations of energy that register upon your consciousness which will enable you to describe details concerning an object and its history or even the history of its owner.

You tune into an object by way of your subconscious. Psychometry is just one of many ways of doing this. It falls under "clairsentience," meaning clear feeling, and "clairvoyance," meaning clear vision. This enables you to see things in a clear way.

Scientists say we have five senses and we may even have a sixth sense. This is where the term "extrasensory perception" came from. It means we have an extra sense with which we can perceive things our other senses don't notice. When we heighten this sense, or fine-tune it, we become aware of unseen forces and vibrations invisible to our normal, everyday senses of sight and sound. When we become aware of these unseen forces, we think we are weird. In fact, all we are doing is becoming aware of our own abilities to see things we were totally unaware of before.

The entire universe reverberates in and through all animate and so-called inanimate objects.

Psychometry can be deep. It can be as deep as you would like it to be. Yet it always remains simple. It dates as far back as the Kabala and probably came from its teaching. Native Americans have always embraced psychometry. Although if you asked them if they do psychometry, they would not know what you are talking about, but if you asked them if they talk to rocks or trees then they would know what you were talking about.

In this book, you will learn how to work with symbols. After reading the basics, you can easily start to use psychometry.

We all have many hopes and fears, longings and frustrations that we have developed in the course of growing up in this hectic society. No matter the culture in which you were raised, there is bound to be some sort of stress. You have problems you would like to solve or resolve. Whatever the particular situation in which you find yourself, good, bad, or indifferent, you would not be human if you had not deep in your heart a desire for a greater measure of freedom---at least greater than you now enjoy.

The greater freedom is precisely what you experience when you gain skill in using psychometry or in learning to read with any other psychic abilities. I can read with many and so can you.

All you have to do is practice and practice until it becomes part of your thinking and knowing. Program it into that computer-like brain of yours until it is part of you. If you don't practice, it will become boring to you, but if you begin to use it on yourself and with your friends, you will find it to be a blessing in your daily life. In the early stages you will be required to put a little effort and a great deal of persistence into it.

Psychometry, like any other form of psychic phenomena, is based on a principle of mental activity common to everyone. It is something we had in early childhood but have lost on the way to becoming the technical-minded grown-up society that we all are to some degree. There is nothing new or unfamiliar in psychometry, only in the application of it in our daily lives.

We must remember —all our basic thinking is done in pictures or symbols. We usually see things before we say them. Mental images form in our mind and we then begin labeling them with words. Even someone blind since birth has a mental image in his or her head before he or she speaks. When we go to school, we learn to put too much faith in language and words. Consequently, we have left the power of our vision by the wayside. Through disuse, we have lost our abilities to create.

Our imaginary mind is our true nature. The word "imagination" is really slang. By saying "imaging" over and over, it lost its true meaning. In reality, there is no such word as imagining. The true word is imaging. If I tell you something, you create the mental picture or image of it in your mind. But if I tell you to imagine something, then it is not quite real. Imaging is real; imagining is not. By losing our awareness of it, we have lost our power of vision. This came about through disuse.

If you have a problem in learning psychometry, it is probably because of our haste in using words without having a mental image of them. We tend to use words too fast without placing mental pictures with the words. We create many problems in our daffy lives by using words too often.

I once met a nun who wanted a reading from me. Before she would let me read her, she wanted to say a prayer and then use her rosary beads. The first thing I noticed was that she said the prayer very fast; when she did her rosary, she was speaking even faster.  She could not say it fast enough.  The rosary and the prayer did not have genuine energy in them because she was not putting any into them.

You cannot create mental pictures in your head as fast as you can say words. I believe if you say the rosary once a week, very slowly, and create a mental picture with the words, you will be creating a prayer with far more power than you could by saying it quickly everyday.

Any initial difficulty you may have in learning to use psychometry may be traced to the bad habit of using words too hastily without being sure these word labels are attached to real pictures.

In the beginning I would like you to sit very comfortably.  To use psychometry and be accurate, you will need to spend at least five minutes in meditation first.  Practice as often as you can with friends.

Hold an article in your hand---a ring, watch, or keys should do at first---that belongs to someone close to you, such as a relative or a friend. In a short while you will be adept at doing this with perfect strangers. Hold the article while you meditate. When you finish meditating, rub your fingers over the object very slowly. Think of this object as having a soul (an electromagnetic energy field or an aura). Ask the soul of this article to reveal something to you. Then pause for a moment, the same way you do when you call someone up on the telephone and ask a question. You simply pause, hesitate, and wait for the answer to come to you.

The answer will come in one or two of many different forms, such as a mental picture, a thought, an idea, a word, or a deep-down gut feeling. You may even hear or smell something. You do not know which faculty will start to develop first. The most important thing is to be calm, relaxed, and to wait for the answer.

## ALLOW IT TO HAPPEN

## LET IT HAPPEN

Remember, never let your mind project an answer, but simply let the answer come to you. You will be amazed at the accuracy of your psychic impressions or perceptions.

The wise man or woman who invented psychometry hit upon a simple way to overcome the difficulties that beset every person who tries to control his or her mind. For thousands of years it has been known that extraordinary powers are latent in every human being and the powers may be directed by anyone who can keep his or her mind from wandering. Thus, we have whole libraries of books about concentration, and the more we read, the more it seems concentration must be very, very difficult. I believe we are very close to death's door when we can keep a single image before the mind's eye for just a few moments. Think of how hard this is to do. Can you hold a single image in your mind for a few minutes or even one whole minute? It is very difficult to accomplish this without external aids.

Hindus and Buddhists call visual meditative devices "mandalas." A mandala is a picture drawn or painted on paper, used as an aid for concentration. I teach people how to read pictures by drawing pictures. Usually, a mandala is an image of God, an image of a spiritual being, or an enlightening picture. I believe this is the reason Tarot cards were originally created to use for meditation, to open the mind's eye and for spiritual growth. It was only later in history did we begin to use the deck of cards for readings.

Psychometry is a device, which, if used properly, will create mental pictures in your mind and will eventually open up your mind to a new awareness of your destiny. It will make you more understanding of what life is all about.

If you hold an article in your hand and meditate on it for five minutes or longer, your state of consciousness will automatically begin to come into attunement with the consciousness of high spiritual beings or even to the depths of the inner school, or inner mind, which is your higher self. You may not become aware of this for a long time, however. I tell you this because some people become aware immediately. Patience and perseverance will be greatly rewarded in due time.

What I want you to do now is hold an article in your hand, gaze at it, think about it, and feel it. Focus all of your attention on it and all its details. For instance, if it is a ring, look at the article very carefully and take in all its details. If you see anything that seems important or arouses your curiosity, make note of it and then ask yourself, "What does this mean." Sooner or later you will come up with the answer and it is almost always exactly right. Even if it feels like it has no importance, just say what you feel. The true answer always comes from within. If the answer doesn't, it comes from the conscious or left side of the brain and it will almost always be wrong. The answer for everything you need to know for any problem in your life always comes from within.

I am not teaching you psychometry, but merely guiding you into it. You are becoming aware of something you already know. I am simply making you aware of it. All I want to teach you is awareness. During the first few weeks, the results may not be particularly impressive, although some times remarkable reactions are experienced from the very beginning. As a rule, though, the effect of psychometric practice is cumulative rather than immediate.

We all have this ability. We just aren't always aware of it. I haven't found anyone yet to whom I couldn't teach this awareness, if he or she was truly interested. Just open yourself up to what is written here. We all have this knowledge inside us, and all you have to do is find the right technique and apply it.

The secret lies within the spirit and the spirit is impersonal. It doesn't select, evaluate, discern, or even judge material. Whatever your body mind thinks and feels, the spirit delivers into your life. Whatever you ask, it will give and it will perform whenever your conscious feeds information into it.

To determine the outcome of your thinking, remember what you project. We can determine the desirable outcome of our next experience, so we must program our mind constructively and positively. Enough can't be said about the mind and I will bring it up again and again. But for now, let's get on with psychometry.

Everything has a soul, which can be visible to the naked eye. Scientists say that in order for you to see any visible object with your eyes, it must be moving. You, in fact, cannot see anything that is standing still. The objects, any material object---whether it is your own body, a car, or the earth---is vibrating violently. The violence is only an appearance, since everything is really in perfect rhythm and accord. These same objects that appear to be standing still, or appear to be solid, are made up of many molecules and atoms that vibrate in motion.

There is an energy (an electromagnetic energy field) that holds these molecules and atoms together, giving us the illusion that we are seeing an object that is standing still. Everything visible to the naked eye, then, is an illusion. And the strange thing about all of this is that our minds control, to a certain degree, the ebb and flow of these same molecules and atoms that are giving us the illusion.

Our minds, therefore, create everything around us. And this electromagnetic energy field (I prefer to call it the soul or aura) is the substance that holds everything in this universe together. This energy field, or soul, is in everything animate and inanimate. It is in our bodies and the bodies of all things manifest.

So, when you tune into an object, you are not really tuning into the object, but rather into the soul of the object. You can receive all knowledge of the object through the soul. This same soul can tell you about everything and everyone that has come in contact with it. This soul can be the soul of a rock, a boat, or a person---anything.

Yes, everything you see with your eyes contains a soul. So what is real? The physical things you see with your eyes or the non-physical things you perceive?

Take a minute to ponder this soul. It is everything and it is everywhere. It is all things visible and invisible. Could this soul of the universe be God, or is it the life-blood of God? If these things are so, then you can definitely see God. It contains all knowledge, yet it never projects this knowledge. You can perceive this knowledge magnetically but never electrically. This is why you have to learn to meditate, so that you can first become aware of this soul, and then you can learn to see it.

Let me show you how to see an aura, or soul. Find a white wall and stand with your back to it. Place a mirror in front of you and look at yourself. Now gaze at your forehead just below the hairline. Allow your eyes to become still and relaxed. Keep staring at your forehead and at the same time become aware of the glow around your body with your peripheral vision. At first you will see a white glow. Then, relax your mind a little more and you soon will see a slight color. You can attain this same vision by holding your hand up. If you continue to gaze at your aura, you will soon see the color become more and more vivid. With a little practice, you will start seeing different colors. Color is energy, and each color has a different meaning. I discuss this in my recent book *Creative Dreams*.

In 1991 Tracey Leonard and his wife Lana invited me to their home in Colorado. He reminded me of a reading I had done back in 1983. Tracey is the equipment editor for Tennis Magazine. I had given Lana a reading back then and she took me up to Tracy's office. She was telling Tracy how good I was when he suddenly proclaimed that he did not believe in psychics. She told him to give me something that I could tune into. He handed me a tennis racquet and I held it close to my head and proceeded to tell him what I saw.

I told Tracy that I saw a tall man with dark hair and that he was thin. I told him that if he could make a few small changes in his play, he would become the best player in the world. In fact, I saw him winning the French Open that year. I said he would go on to Germany. There I saw him win diamonds, jewels, and gold. Tracy asked me if I picked up a name while holding the racquet. I told him that his name was Ivan Lendl.

Ivan Lendl did win the French Open in 1983 as well as the German Open. He was awarded a solid gold tennis ball with diamonds and jewels in it.

You do not need to learn psychometry to give such a reading, though, but it is a great catalyst. About ten years ago, I was giving a lady a reading and told her that she was going to witness a robbery. It would be in her bank and she would see the whole thing. I even told her that she would be the one to call the police. It happened just that way. I did not use psychometry in that reading. Psychometry is a valuable tool, but you can do the same without using it.

The person that I was reading has a soul just like an object. I did not have to touch the person's body with my hand. I touched it with my mind. You can do the same thing over the telephone. You can tune into the person with your mind over the wire. Sometimes when I am reading a person and they ask me about another person, I tune into that person without any contact at all. Of course, I believe I am tuning into and through the person that is sitting there. The soul knows everything, including your very own soul.

There are certain keys to follow in order to "LET" you tune in.

Think, meditate, and ponder on this word "LET" for a while.

Remember, once again, that the left hemisphere of your brain is the seat of your conscious mind, the body mind. Your body mind is the doer; it is electrical in nature. It projects thoughts, analyzes, reasons, and rationalizes. It is positive and masculine in nature.

The right hemisphere is the seat of your subconscious mind, the spirit mind. It is feminine and magnetic. It is the receiver, the knower, the creator; and it is passive. So, when I say, "let," I mean you must use the spirit mind; not the body mind.

So start using the word "LET." Begin by holding an article that belongs to someone, preferably something such as jewelry or something worn close to the body, a ring, watch, or necklace. If you don't have jewelry, try keys or even clothing.

Hold the article in your hand, feel it, and rub it gently. LET it tell you something. By holding it and rubbing it gently, it will draw all of your attention to it. At first, you will be thinking of this article strictly with your body mind. But remember, you cannot think of a single object consciously for more than a few minutes. If you keep rubbing it, soon your body mind will stop projecting thoughts. You will start daydreaming and your conscious thoughts will switch to subconscious thoughts or your left-brain thinking will switch to right-brain thinking. All the while, keep rubbing the article. I prefer to use my thumb. It seems to pick up more than my other.

Now ask the article to reveal something to you about its owner. Remember to be totally calm and relaxed. Take a deep breath and become at ease with yourself. Now just wait for the answer. It will soon come to you through one of your senses. I am talking about your refined senses - clairvoyance, clear vision; clairsentience, clear feeling; and clairaudience, to hear clearly. These are your inner senses, not your outer physical senses.

You never know how you will begin to develop, but most people begin with clairsentience. This intuitive message may come through any of these faculties. It may come in the form of a thought or a feeling about the person or you may even hear something by way of your inner ear. Your inner ear receives messages the same way you receive ideas. In fact, all ideas are nothing more than clairaudient or clairvoyant messages. Remember to be alert and absolutely still.

Another way to practice psychometry, which may be even more effective, is to hold the article either on or close to your forehead. Your forehead contains a massive nerve center just above and between the eyes. This place is called the "third eye" and is extremely sensitive. By holding the article there, you will begin to open up your psychic sight much sooner. Just ask once again, *I desire to know something about the person who owns this article.* The vibrations will soon start to come. Pause, wait, and let it all happen. Be especially attentive. Whatever comes, TRUST IT because you won't know if what you have received is true or not until you tell it to the person.

Now try this. Take someone by the hand and hold it gently. Remember, always be sincere about what you receive. (Of course, the person must be aware of why you are holding his or her hand; otherwise, you might frighten the person.) While holding the hand, let something flow into your head, a thought or a feeling. Then immediately say to the person whatever comes to you, either by way of sight or sound or feel. The first impression is always the right impression.

You will always be correct. However, if you pick up a secret, the person may not confess it to you. This is why I always stress that you must be honest, sincere, and gentle with the person.

It is important to keep practicing. Above all, do not worry if you seem to have failed. Never go by appearances. Trust your inner judgment.

Once you have the basics of psychometry in your mind, you can begin to use it in many different ways. For instance, you don't necessarily have to hold something to tune into it. You simply tune in by just thinking about it. (Of course when I say thinking, I mean perceiving.) You should develop the first method first, however. Then try focusing your mind on an object and let the thoughts flow into your head. You will begin to know exactly what I mean just by practicing this method. Later, you will not become attached to just one method. Besides, sometimes you cannot hold an article, because the person may live far away. But you can project your mind to a far away place and the thoughts or feelings will soon flow into your consciousness.

Remember, you always have a body mind. It will always interfere and sometimes even project itself unto the message you have received. Then the message will be either colored with untruth or may not be true at all. This is the biggest oversight of all for many psychics. It is the main reason most psychics are right only a percentage of the time. Never allow your body mind to get into your psychic messages. The only way you can keep your conscious-analytical mind out is to always remain calm and relaxed and do not try to impress anyone or try to prove anything.
 Remain in the meditative mood as though you are daydreaming.

Here is another method. Have someone pick a flower and let it tell you something. As I have previously explained, a flower has a soul just as you do. Its soul will reveal something to you about the person that picked it. There are other ways of tuning into the flower, but you should use psychometry first.

Hold the flower closely and observe it. Notice how many petals it has. You are now bringing numerology into the reading. Count the petals. Here is a brief synopsis of the numbers from one to nine.

One: always means new beginnings.

Two: the scales, or balance, or going from one extreme to another.

Three: the artist, creator, inventor.

Four: all aspects of the body mind, hard work.

Five: movement, travel, and communication.

Six: personal possessions, love and romance on all levels, jewelry.

Seven: a spiritual number that contains magic in the sense of bringing good fortune, a most sacred number spiritually.

Eight: the executive, money, riches, a position of power, authority, and being the boss.

Nine: the number of completion: finishing up some thing: rules, religion, the higher mind.

For more information on numbers, look for my forthcoming book entitled *Electricity in Numbers*.

Now, once again, hold the flower in your hand and let it revolve by turning it in a circle. BE ALERT. Do you notice anything? Are you sure? Did you notice the color of the flower? Colors have meanings, also, because color is energy and it is very significant. Also, watch for my forthcoming book on color and auras entitled *The Rainbow of Light*. I am process of writing a series of books that will be of aid to you. Here is a brief overview of color meanings. , I am only giving you the positive colors. There are no negative colors in flowers.

Red: energy, strength, magnetism, and personal energy.

Blue: someone is loyal (true blue); spiritual, honest, and sincere; the spirit body.

Green: nature, the physical body, sensuality and growth, the emotional body.

Yellow: the mind, intellect; artistic, psychic, opportunity, a sensitive person.

Violet: The higher mind, spirit; healing of the soul, and all consuming color, a higher ray of light and will consume any negative colors.

Orange: Energy in a mental way, kindness, passion, and compassion.

White: Pure and clean, contains all colors and therefore means perfection. Contains all attributes of all other colors. Perfect white becomes invisible to the naked eye.

Black: The absence of color or energy, yet all colors eventually spring from the color black; all energy comes from blackness as well. Color and energy are synonymous. Walter Russell said that the CREATOR comes from the still black universe, and that everything else is an expression of the Creator, and must come from out of the cold black universe of unknowing. If someone wears a lot of black, they are looking for major changes in their life; black means change. Did you ever see a black flower?

Hold the flower in your hand and let the color tell you something about the person. Use psychometry along with some of the symbols I am teaching you and you will become quite proficient. Observe the symbols. Everything you do in life is a symbol locked into your subconscious mind (spirit mind). Everything you see with your eyes is a symbol, also locked into your subconscious mind.

Even when you dream at night, very rarely do you dream actual events. You usually dream in symbols. This is because you are awake more hours than you are asleep and your spirit mind (subconscious mind) fires symbols at you very rapidly. This is because you are creating new events for tomorrow and you are balancing things you didn't balance while you were awake.

You rehearse or create coming events as faraway as twenty years from now. Learn how to read your spirit mind and you will learn what is in store for you tomorrow. This is all that a psychic does. He or she reads your spirit mind, nothing more than that. Actually, no one can read the future, not even a prophet. There is no such thing. When a prophet or psychic appears to be reading the future, all he or she is doing is reading something that is already created within the mind, either yours or the Universal Mind. You simply create the future in your sleep, and when you are seemingly awake, you are just acting out what you created when you were asleep.

Now, let's look at the symbol of the flower. For instance, suppose the flower has a short stem. This may mean the person does things in small ways, short-term experiences. It also means he or she lacks substance and is not firmly rooted in his or her affairs. If the stem is long, the opposite is true. Suppose the flower is short, yet full of the color red. This shows the person having much strength, much energy, yet tires easily. It shows he or she is hyper, scattered, and likes to do things in a big way, but may not always succeed. The person may lack perseverance.

Everything you do is a symbol. The car you drive, the job you have, and the clothes you wear; even the color of your clothes, your car, and your house. Yes, everything, including the food you eat and the company you keep. Everything you say, think, touch, and feel---all are symbolic in your life. Observe the lines on your face, hands, and even your feet. They show the life you live, whether it is stressful, happy, uneventful, or full of life. You are an expression of your life. Stand in a mirror and observe.

The most important key to your life is awareness. The most important key in psychometry or the psychic field is awareness. Someday, we will all become aware of everything we do, say, think, act, and react in all situations. When this occurs, we will all have happiness, balance, and abundance.

We will then become more creative in our thinking and actions, in work and play, in relationships with others, and especially in our own personal situation.

Remember one thing. The underlying cause for all things visible and invisible is spirit. Spirit is everywhere and in all things. Awareness is the key to spirit. Awareness is the key to all doors of knowledge. It exists in the solitude of your soul. The words of man usually die within the borders of his dreams. Think of the essence of what I am saying to you, not my words. The spirit of the universe lies between my words. Let it enter into your heart, and into the meadows of your mind, and into your awareness. Feel elated, uplifted and inspired, for inspiration is when God is talking to you.

Do not get lost in my words, for words are like phantoms rising from within all things. Once spoken, or even written, they will create great changes. Silence, therefore, brings great peace. This peace can only descend on the man called the dreamer. With the dreamer, matter turns into spirit and the identity of all things become known or revealed. All matter is controlled by spirit. The dreamer becomes at one with his spirit. Spirit is everywhere. It is in the trees, rocks, earth, sky, and clouds; yes, even in you and me.

As you hold the flower in your hand, close your eyes, breath deeply and rhythmically. Ask the flower to reveal something to you. Be very patient. Pause for a moment and reflect on the flower. Soon something will begin to happen. You may receive an idea. This idea will come in a thought, the form of a mental image or picture, or like a dream. It may be the form of a person, place, or thing. When you get the form of something, ask the flower to tell you what the form means because the form may simply be a symbol. Let your mind be receptive; there may be something going on in the person's life now that may be emotional, mental, or physical. Erase your desire to know just one thing about the person and you will know two things.

Pay no attention to the scattered thoughts that are going out of your head. The thoughts coming into your head will not be scattered, although, at times, they may give that appearance. The thoughts coming into your head may take many forms; sound being one of them. Did you ever suddenly hear someone call out your name when you were all alone? You turned around and no one was there?

So, when you hold the flower, be prepared for anything. The quieter and the calmer your mind becomes, the more receptive you will become.

When you hold the flower, focus on its beauty and aroma. Allow the beauty to flow into your entire being. Absorb it. Become the flower. Feel your spirit flow inside the flower. Let yourself be caught up in the aura, in its entire being. Try this every time you go into the woods, field, or by a lake or stream. The noted scientist George Washington Carver went into the forest at 4 a.m. everyday to commune with the flowers. He loved the flowers and the trees. He always wore a flower in his buttonhole. He communed with the Universal Spirit, the Creator (as he preferred to call him) through a flower. He believed that if you love a flower enough, it will reveal its secrets to you and it will talk back to you. When it talks back, it talks to you in thoughts, feelings, ideas, and inspiration. Carver always strove to remain natural and relaxed. He believed his inventions came through him from the infinite forces in the universe and never so well as when he was relaxed.

He understood, as I do, that we all have inherent power if only we believe. The secret lies in the belief in the Universal Mind, or God. God promises us in the Bible that we can have all these gifts and abilities. In fact, we already do. One day, Carver was sent a flower from a chemist in South Carolina. It was suffering from a peculiar disease that was threatening most of the flowers in that state. Carver healed the flower and saved the flowers in that state. This gentle man, this kind and loving person, spoke to the flowers and allowed the flowers to speak back to him. He spoke to the flower about the peanut and was given three hundred uses for it, including using peanut oil to massage the legs of infantile paralysis victims and thus cure them.

The following passage captures the essence of Carver's search for spiritual understanding:

*One morning, while walking in the forest, a flower spoke to him and asked him what he wanted to know. He replied, "Oh Mr. Creator, please tell me what the universe was made for." The Creator replied, "You want to know too much for that little mind of yours. Ask for something more your size." So he asked, "Dear Mr. Creator, tell me what man was made for." Again the Creator replied, "Little man, you still keep asking too much. Cut down the extent of your request and improve on the intent." So, then George said, "Please, Mr. Creator, will you tell me why the peanut was made?" "That's better, but even the peanut is infinite and you could never completely know it," the Creator replied. So George asked, "Mr. Creator, can I make milk out of the peanut?" "What kind of milk do you want, good Jersey milk or just plain boarding house milk?" "Good Jersey milk." And then the Creator taught him how to take the peanut apart and put it back together again. And out of that process came forth a multitude of products: printer's ink, face powder, butter, shampoo, creosote, vinegar, a dandruff cure, instant coffee, dyes, rubberoid compounds, soaps, and wood stains. Carver was one of the* first to invent synthetic fabrics. He even prepared a complete meal once, with everything made from the peanut. All this from Love. (The Man Who Spoke With the Flowers by Glenn Clark, currently out of print)

Suppose you have gone through life feeling unloved or unlovable. This becomes a deep-seated, subconscious pattern, which has manifested in your environment. It expresses itself in your relationships with family, friends, and business associates. We are in continuous contact with each other on all subconscious levels. If we feel unloved, we call from ourselves and others we meet, the type of contact that brings rejection. Change the inner patterns and you change the relationships from unhappy to happy ones. Psychometry will help you to do this. The practice of psychometry helps you become aware of who and what you are, why you are here, and where you are going. But this is a metaphor, a riddle, solve it and you will inherit the earth. It is very simple.

As you learn to live and feel the positive states of your conscious mind, you transform your own personality. It is very subtle at first, but it soon manifests in your everyday life. It happens gradually, but it will happen and people will start to take notice. You will start to attract things into your life. Psychometry is not a game. It is very real. It gives you a greater ability to change your total environment. If you want to enhance this, affirmations together with mental pictures will be very effective.

The practice of psychometry is designed to bring about transcendence, first of the soul, then in the physical body and subsequently in your everyday life. It can also eventually bring abundance into your life because it teaches you to have absolute faith in the images and thought forms you are getting. These transcendent changes are required for mental, spiritual, and physical growth. It is will work if you will only allow it to seep into your spirit mind.

The next time you sit by a stream or a lake, feel the energy of the water. Absorb it. Feel it. You will soon begin to know what I mean. Have you ever gone outside on a clear, mild, and breezy day when the temperature was perfect and you felt it was fantastic just to be alive? Do you feel absolutely exhilarated and full of energy? The next time that happens, be aware of everything around you. You will feel so full of life because you have become in tune with all of nature.

Primitive man worshipped certain trees and flowers. The Indians of the Amazon worshipped a God that led you around in circles when you were lost and protected you when you were in harmony with the forest. They considered the tree to be inhabited by a spirit, or a god, and thus it became sacred. Many times, when I am counseling someone, I find myself gazing at a tree in the same way a person gazes at a crystal ball. Crystal gazing is the same as daydreaming. When you daydream, you go into a light trance and you find yourself off somewhere. The only difference between a crystal gazer and a daydreamer is the daydreamer goes wherever his mind takes him. A crystal gazer directs his mind to wherever he wants it to go.

Whenever I gaze upon a tree, I focus on something that I want to know, or need information about. The tree responds and gives it to me. I have had a love for trees since I was a little boy. Even now when I gaze upon a tree, I become like a little boy once again. I feel much reverence for trees and I feel love flowing from them, as well, even more than I do from flowers.

The following subject about birthday trees recently came to me by way of email. So I thought I would share it with you because it is so important.

Subject: Which tree does your birthday fall?

**Apple Tree, the Love (Dec. 23 to Jan. 1, June 25 to July 4)**
Of slight build, lots of charm, appeal, and attraction, pleasant aura, flirtatious, adventurous, sensitive, always in love, wants to love and be loved, faithful and tender partner, very generous, scientific talents, lives for today, a carefree philosopher with imagination.

**Fir Tree, the Mysterious (Jan. 2 to Jan. 11, July 5 to July 14)**
Extraordinary taste, dignity, cultivated airs, loves anything beautiful, moody, stubborn, tends toward egoism but cares for those close to it, rather modest, very ambitious, talented, industrious, un-content lover, many friends, many foes, very reliable.

**Elm Tree, the Noble-Mindedness (Jan. 12 to Jan. 24, July 15 to July 25)**

Pleasant shape, tasteful clothes, modest demands, tends to not forgive mistakes, cheerful, likes to lead but not to obey, honest and faithful partner, tends to a know-all-attitude and making decisions for others, noble-minded, generous, good sense of humor, practical.

### Cypress, the Faithfulness (Jan. 25 to Feb. 3, July 26 to Aug.4)

Strong, muscular, adaptable, takes what life has to give, happy content, optimistic, needs enough money and acknowledgement, hates loneliness, passionate lover which cannot be satisfied, faithful, quick-tempered, unruly, pedantic, and careless.

### Poplar, the Uncertainty (Feb. 4 to 8, May 1 to 14, Aug. 5 to 13)

Looks very decorative, no self-confident behavior, only courageous if necessary, needs goodwill and pleasant surroundings, very choosy, often lonely, great animosity, artistic nature, good organizer, tends toward philosophy, reliable in any situation, takes partnership seriously.

### Cedar, the Confidence (Feb. 9 to Feb. 18, Aug. 14 to Aug. 23)

Of rare beauty, knows how to adapt, likes

luxury, of good health not in the least shy, tends to look down on others, self-confident, determined, impatient, wants to impress others, many talents, industrious, healthy optimism, waits for the one true love, able to make quick decisions.

**Pine Tree, the Particularity (Feb. 19 to Feb. 28, Aug. 24 to Sep. 2)**
Loves agreeable company, very robust, knows how to make life comfortable, very active, natural, good companion but seldom friend, falls easily in love but its passion burns out quickly, gives up easily, many disappointments till it finds its ideal situation, trustworthy, practical.

**Weeping Willow, the Melancholy (March 1 to March 10, Sep. 3 to Sep. 12)**
beautiful but full of melancholy, attractive, very empathic, loves anything beautiful and tasteful, loves to travel, dreamer, restless, capricious, honest, can be influenced but is not easy to live with, demanding, good intuition, suffers in love but finds sometimes an anchoring partner.

**Lime Tree, the Doubt (March 11 to March 20, Sep. 13 to Sep. 22)**
Accepts what life dishes out in a composed

way, hates fighting, stress, and labor, tends toward laziness and idleness, soft and relenting, makes sacrifices for friends, many talents but not tenacious enough to make them blossom, often wailing and complaining, very jealous, loyal.

## Hazelnut Tree, the Extraordinary (March 22 to March 31, Sep 24 to Oct.3)

Charming, undemanding, very understanding, knows how to make an impression, active fighter for social causes, popular, moody and capricious lover, honest and tolerant partner, precise sense of judgment.

## Rowan Tree, the Sensitivity (Apr. 1 to Apr. 10, Oct. 4 to Oct. 13)

Full of charm, cheerful, gifted, without egoism, likes to draw attention, loves life, motion, unrest and even complications, both dependent and independent, good tastes, artistic, passionate, emotional, good company, does not forgive.

## Maple Tree, Independence of Mind (Apr. 11 to Apr. 20, Oct. 14 to Oct. 23)

No ordinary person, full imagination and originality, shy and reserved, ambitious, proud, self-respect, hungers for new experiences, sometimes nervous, many complexes, good memory, learns easily, complicated love life, wants to impress.

**Walnut Tree, the Passion (Apr. 21 to Apr. 30, Oct. 24 to Nov. 11)**
Unrelenting, strange and full of contrasts, often egoistic, aggressive, noble, broad horizon, unexpected reactions, spontaneous, unlimited ambition, no flexibility, difficult and uncommon partner, not always liked but often admired, ingenious strategist, very jealous and passionate, no compromises.

**Chestnut Tree, the Honesty (May 15 to May 24, Nov. 12 to Nov. 21)**
Of unusual beauty, does not want to impress, well-developed sense of justice, vivacious, interested, a born diplomat, but irritable and sensitive in company—often due to a lack of self-confidence, sometimes acts superior, feels not understood, loves only once, has difficulties in finding a partner.

**Ash Tree, the Ambition (May 25 to June 3, Nov. 22 to Dec. 1)**
Uncommonly attractive, vivacious, impulsive, demanding, does not care for criticism, ambitious, intelligent, talented, likes to play with its fate, can be egoistical, very reliable and trustworthy, faithful and prudent lover,

sometimes brains rule over heart, but takes partnership very seriously.

### Hornbeam Tree, the Good Taste (June 4 to June 13, Dec. 2 to Dec. 11)
Of cool beauty, cares for its looks and condition, good tastes, tends toward egoism, makes life as comfortable as possible, leads reasonably, disciplined life, looks for kindness, an emotional partner and acknowledgement, dreams of unusual lovers, is seldom happy with feelings, mistrusts most people, is never sure of its decisions, very conscientious.

### Fig Tree, the Sensibility (June 14 to June 23, Dec. 12 to Dec. 21)
Very strong, a bit self-willed, independent, does not allow contradiction or arguments, loves life, its family, children and animals, a bit of a butterfly, good sense of humor, likes idleness and laziness, of practical talent and intelligence.

### Oak Tree, the Robust Nature (March 21)
Courageous, strong, unrelenting, independent, sensible, does not love changes, keeps its feet on the ground, person of action.

### Birch, the Inspiration (June 24)

Vivacious, attractive, elegant, friendly, unpretentious, modest, does not like anything in excess, abhors the vulgar, loves life in nature and in calmness, not very passionate, full of imagination, little ambition, creates a calm and content mind.

**Olive Tree, the Wisdom (Sept. 23)**
Loves sun, warmth and kind feelings, reasonable, balanced, avoids aggression and violence, tolerant, cheerful, calm, well-developed sense of justice, sensitive, empathic, free of jealousy, loves to read and the company of sophisticated people.

**Beech Tree, the Creative (Dec. 22)**
Has good taste, concerned about its looks, materialist, good organization of life and career, economical, good leader, takes no unnecessary risks, reasonable, splendid lifetime companion, keen on keeping fit (diets, sports, etc.).

This is, in fact, what all psychics do. They simply direct their energy in the direction they want to pursue. If I want to tune in to you, I just direct my mind and energy in your direction. I can do this without ever having met or seen you. All I would need is your name or month and day of birth; I don't even need the year you were born.

Or, if someone showed me a picture of you, I could tell you many things about yourself and probably know you better than you do yourself.

Or, I could use psychometry on any object that belongs to you because everything is energy, including us. All I have to do is direct my energy in the direction of your energy and I can tune in to you and perhaps even find you.

The Sioux, or rather the Lakota, as they prefer to be called (the word Sioux is French and means cut-throat), thought it sacred to bury their dead by wrapping them in blankets and putting them in trees. Indians in California would hollow out giant redwoods and put their dead inside so their spirit would be captured by the tree and would be preserved and protected there. They thought the soul would enter the tree at death.

The Hindu Bayudas worship their ancestors in groves of Saj trees. In Southern Nigeria, it is customary to have one big tree within the village to worship. In New Guinea, the villages have a sacred death tree. The Patagonians,

Greeks, Vikings, and Persians all claim man originally came from the trees. The Druids were known as the "Tree Priests" and worshipped the oak tree. To prophesy, they would tune into the leaves, using psychometry. They called the forest spirits the "Oak Maidens."

At one time, the Arabs worshipped the acacia tree as a form of the Love Goddess. Ancient Greeks thought the best place to study was under an old oak tree. Many religious beliefs included "stone spirits" and "flower spirits." The Lakota worship in the Stone People's Lodge. At Findhorn, Scotland, there is a community founded on belief in these same flower spirits, sometimes known as elves, gnomes, and fairies. The God Pan rules over them all. Spirit permeates everything. The Vikings would tune into the Rune stones for spiritual counsel. You can do the same thing. When you can tune-in to one thing you can tune-in to all things. There is a message waiting for you everywhere. You can have the answer or solution to any problem anytime you need it. Look for the symbols. Look into the clouds.

There is a profound mystical reason for this. Yet, you should be on your guard against paying too much attention to any one symbol over another one, especially in the beginning.

Every symbol is some aspect of you, as well as of the person who owns the article that you hold. Remember, when reading someone's article, the subject matter is always of that person, only sometimes can it be applied to you. No matter what a picture looks like, it will invariably be for the person you are reading. If you are reading for yourself (This takes much practice, no matter what a picture or mental image may look like.), it will always be about you. Nothing interests you more in life than your own self. In reality, self is all there is.

If you are moody or have some kind of psychological complex, you may not be willing to admit that nothing interests you as much as yourself. If you are of sound mind, you know this to be true and will readily admit it. If you are an old soul or an advanced soul, there is nothing else that interests you. Everyone and everything is a mirrored image of your own self. All wisdom is the mature experience of those who obey this injunction: Know thyself.

I will give you more steps, but first I think that you should know that you are reading this book because something inside of you has awakened. It is a light that you have been seeking since the dark ages of man. It is a gradual transition in your thinking and you will slowly become aware of your true self. You are becoming aware that your body is not you, that you are an immortal soul and are gradually losing your past thoughts of being a mortal person and are seeking the light that is within you. A mortal person does not and cannot know who he or she is, nor can a mortal person know God. In the long ages past, you have been living for your body. You have been taking whatever you can for your body and always seeking and creating sensual pleasure. Of course, this is all that your body can do, is seek and enjoy pleasure.

Your soul, however, which is very gentle and subtle, always seeks happiness. Pleasure is of the senses; happiness is always of the spirit. Whenever you have pleasure, you will always be let down. Whenever you have happiness, it is enduring and lasts forever.

# Chapter 4

# The Quest of the Higher Self

You are becoming aware of your own immortality. You are among the few. Some eighty to ninety percent of the masses are still in the dark ages, the barbaric stage of man. But you will unfold, however, and grow into the awareness stage. This is the stage where you become born again. You are becoming aware of the spiritual nature of man. Even if you have had just a slight glimpse of the light, you have become forever changed. You now need to go within, to seek more of that light that is within you. It will come more and more often. You may at times feel as though you have found your soul, or you soul's destiny. It is like a beacon; it gets stronger and then sometimes you may feel that it is fading. You will be inspired and uplifted each time it comes. Sometimes, in extremely rare cases, the light will come for all illumination. If this happens, you will go past the next level of your soul's evolution in consciousness, which is the genius level. I classify each level of the consciousness as follows:

<u>Barbaric level</u>: where the masses are today

<u>Awareness level</u>: maybe 7 to 8 percent

<u>Genius level</u>: only a handful

<u>Cosmic Consciousness</u>: perhaps a few people since the dawn of man

<u>Christ Consciousness</u>: I only know of a few; perhaps there were more, Jesus being the greatest Krishna (The word Krishna in Sanskrit means: Christ.), Buddha, Melchizedek, Pythagoras, Lao Tsu, Chang Tzu, and perhaps more.

I believe that the masses will go through 12 stages in this evolution. We are in the fourth stage, and soon will be entering the fifth. Actually, we are standing at the gates of the fifth. There are twelve stages and seven levels of consciousness. Two of the seven are not in this material world.

You become whatever you think, or should I say, you create what you see inside of your head. Seeing is believing and seeing is true thinking. If you become what you think, then the masses become what they think. If you can believe this, then you know that we have to stop thinking negatively about the world coming to an end. Nothing ends. It only changes. If we do not like the world as it is, then we must change it. Likewise, if you do not like the way your life is, then change it. Begin by meditating, by going within.

If we all would take into consideration the welfare of all living things, animate and inanimate, then we would be well on the way to world peace. If you decide to try it, you will find an inner peace and you will find happiness.

Higher consciousness, wisdom, and understanding come to you solely through your unfolding of the divine light within.

We are seeking a vision through meditation. Some go off to a mountaintop, while others will go into the ground. I was with Wallace Black Elk back in 1983-84. At that time, he had a big hole in the ground that you were to enter, and there was another hole below that one. After preparing to seek a vision (It usually takes you about a year before you are ready.), you would go through a week of fasting, and daily ceremonies in the sweat lodge. (Purification ceremony) He would lead you in a procession down in the ground. When the lid was closed, you were in the ground with no light and no sound for about 24 hours. If you did not have a vision, then you would prepare for another year and go in the ground for 48 hours, and if you still did not have a vision, then you would go in for 72 hours. And if you still did not have a vision, then you would have to call it off, wait a few years before starting again. I have not met anyone that did not have a vision.

My method is not like the Lakota's. I would take people up into the mountains and camp out for a week. I would then teach them how to tune into a flower, rock, clouds, eyes, etc. Everyone has his or her own way. Seek it and you will find it. It is there waiting for you, and only you.

In November 1988, I took a group of people that watched my television show (appropriately called "Vision Quest" on the TKR Cable out of Warren, New Jersey) to Yucatan, Mexico. We visited the pyramids. Each day we would practice a different form of psychic ability, and with tremendous success. The first day, I would show them how to meditate and to tune-in to inanimate objects---psychometry.

On day two, we went to the pyramids where we had many experiences. I firmly believe that whenever I take a group on a "Vision Quest," they will have a psychic experience. I personally guarantee it. Why? Because I believe that everyone has psychic ability.

One such experience was a during a candle meditation. I went into a trance by the light of the candle. Not only did everyone experience their guides, but also most, if not all, saw their guides superimposed on my face. There was a phenomenal amount of power during that night and everyone was a believer after that. Of course, each day and night was a whole new experience. I will mention a few of them.

While on top of the pyramid of Uzhmul, our Mexican guide told us that it is a tradition to chant the "om." While chanting, we all noticed that the musty smell of the pyramid changed to a sweet aroma. When we finished, I asked each person about his or her experience. Most said they felt like spirits were touching them. Some heard wings flapping, and they thought it was an eagle. Some felt a spiritual uplifting or a blissful feeling.

Later while on the pyramid, two students were practicing Tai Chi. They said that while they were practicing their forms, an energy started to overcome them. They were now doing a form that they were never taught. They said that they were at one with the energy. A crowd gathered around them and marveled while watching their gracefulness. While I was watching them, I thought they were almost floating in the swirls of energy.

Then we visited an ancient Mayan ruin on the beach at Cancun. We were doing a sunrise meditation, and when we were done, everyone talked about the magnificent colors they had experienced.

You must know that most of the people that went on this trip had not had any psychic experiences before. We also took a video team along with us, and the cinematographer who didn't believe in visions, now was seeing and hearing things that he previously thought were impossible. He also captured some very unusual scenes.

In May 1989, 1 took another group to Sedona, Arizona. It was a phenomenal trip. We started the night off with a meditation, and the next day at breakfast, everybody was smiling. They said that they had so much energy that they stayed up until 3:00 am.

I talked to them about the Lakota, the people of the earth, the same people we call Indian. I explained their ways and traditions as I learned them and talked about the medicine wheel. We then went on a tour of the famous vortexes. Oddly enough, our guide was a full-blooded Indian named Trahiello. He talked about the Native American's way of life and proceeded to do a medicine wheel ceremony. The tour lasted about two hours, and everyone commented on how everything he said, I had said previously. It sounded much better coming from Trahelio. That night we went camping out on Bell Rock. We were told that UFO's were frequently seen there. Well, we didn't see any UFO's but it was a beautiful night and we made our own medicine wheel and had a sound sleep out under the stars.

As you can see, you can meditate anywhere and still have phenomenal experiences. Always expect the unexpected and do not feel that you have to go into a deep trance-like state in order to achieve anything. The secret is in the breathing.

The following are some additional steps to proper breathing, but first you will have to imagine that you are doing this before you actually do it. Remember, seeing is believing. You have to create the meditation in your mind and the rest will follow.

Sit erect, breathing through the nostrils. Imagine that you have three sections in your lungs. Inhale slowly at first, filling the lower section. This is accomplished by distending the diaphragm, which exerts a gentle pressure on the stomach and pushes forward the front wall of the abdomen.

Then, fill the middle section of the lungs by pushing out the lower ribs, breastbone, and chest. Now, fill the top section of the lungs by protruding the upper chest thus lifting the chest. In the final movement, the lower part of the abdomen will be slightly drawn in, which gives the lungs support and also helps to fill the highest part of the lungs.

It may appear by the above description that this kind of breathing consists of three distinct movements. This, however, is not correct. The inhalation is continuous, with the entire chest cavity from the lower diaphragm to the highest point of the chest in the region of the collarbone, being expanded with a uniform movement. Avoid a jerky series of inhalations and strive to attain a steady, continuous action. With practice you will soon overcome the tendency to divide the inhalation into three movements and you will be able to complete the inhalation in a couple of seconds.

Retain the breath a few seconds.

Exhale quite slowly, holding the chest in a firm position and drawing the abdomen in a little and lifting it upward slowly as the air leaves the lungs. When the air is entirely exhaled, relax the chest and abdomen. A little practice will render this part of the exercise easy. The movement once learned, will be performed almost automatically afterwards.

With this method of breathing, all parts of the respiratory apparatus are brought into action and all parts of the lungs, including the most remote air cells, are exercised.

The chest cavity is expanded in all directions. You will notice that the total breath is really a combination of low, middle, and high breaths, succeeding each other rapidly in the order given, in such a manner as to form one uniform, continuous, complete breath. Practice this technique in front of a large mirror and place the hands lightly over the abdomen so you may feel the movements.

The most important thing in meditation is to be relaxed. Don't make it difficult by sitting in an uncomfortable position.

Whatever you desire to do, you can do. Whatever anyone else has done, you can do also. Whatever is accomplishable can be accomplished, if you but desire it. The only reason you may not have done anything remarkable is because you have not been aware of the genius inside of you. Believing makes it so. You can only express whatever you believe. If you watch someone's actions, you are watching his or her beliefs. If you want to learn how to become aware of the genius inside of you, then practice meditation. The secret is in the breathing.

## MILKY-WAY

This form of meditation was given to me by Quanah Parker, Comanche, while I was channeling him in a group meeting. He said to use this method for fulfilling your desires.

Visualize the picture of whatever it is that you want to appear very clearly in your mind. Now fill this image with all of the desire that you can manifest. Create a maximum desire. This is very important.

When you breathe in air, imagine a light outside of you that is a very sticky, strong, very milky, very heavy-like fog. Think of yourself sitting in this fog (a white milky substance which is clear and at the same time not so clear).

There is a very strong spirit that lies behind all things. This same spirit is the substance that we will be calling upon in this milky-way meditation. (This meditation is used to manifest your desires into your life.)

Visualize this substance going into your lungs and there, it attaches itself firmly to you. It flows into your heart and changes your heart from red to white, like a marshmallow. Then see it flowing upward into the brain. It will take at least three breaths to get it into the brain, but eventually it will take only one fluid breath, as you get better.

<u>The seven steps through the Milky-way meditation.</u>

Breathe deeply into your lungs.

Breathe deeply into your heart and bloodstream.

Now take three deep breaths, bringing the substance up into brain.

Now see the picture you desire for yourself or others. Draw the milky white substance into the picture. This gives your creation substance and form.

Now put color in the picture. Do this also with your breath. Imagine that your breath is causing color to fill up your picture. This is energizing your picture. Now it has color and substance, the two ingredients needed in all of creation.

See the picture becoming solidified, as though it is now cast in stone.

Breathe a blue flame into your creation. Now the picture is spiritualized. When you visualize this blue flame flowing into the picture, you are giving life to the picture. This is a great way to create through meditation. Each time you practice this meditation, allow your mind to be creative and inventive. Allow your imagination to flow freely while at the same time you are still following these steps. If you can eventually do this meditation with one fluid motion, you will become a master artist or inventor of your life.

# CIRCLE OF FIRE

My students and I once received the Circle of Fire Meditation from the great Quanah Parker. It is used to cleanse the system.

This great soul also proceeded to give the Ring of Fire meditation to spiritualize the physical body. First, let me give you the steps of the cleansing Circle of Fire Meditation:

Breathe in seven deep breaths through the nostrils, and out through the mouth. Be sure to breathe deeply into the third section of your lungs. (Imagine you are filling up your stomach.)

Now breathe the blue flame into your forehead, or third eye, and with a continuous flow, see the blue flame flowing down into your throat (thyroid and parathyroid glands).

Visualize this blue flame flowing with your next breath down into heart and lungs.

Follow this flame as it proceeds down into the solar plexus.

Breathe it into the navel.

Breathe it into groin.

Breathe it into tailbone.

Inhale this blue flame once again and see it flowing up the spine to the back of head (Pineal gland).

Inhale the flame and see it flow from the back of your head, towards the center of the forehead (third eye).

*Circle of Fire*

Breathe the flame from the forehead out through the right temple.

Breathe this flame from right temple, around the front of the head into the left temple.

Finally, breathe the blue flame back out of your forehead (third eye).

You will stumble with this at first and this meditation works best with someone leading you into it. When you have mastered this meditation, the eleven steps become one. You will be able to do the complete cycle of flame breathing in one breath. Before you can do this physically, you must be able to first see the complete breathing in your mind.

## RING OF FIRE

Breathe in the Ruby Red Flame through the nostrils and into the forehead. Then allow the energy to flow to the back of the head down the spine to the tailbone, into the groin, up into the navel. Continue into the solar plexus, toward the heart, on up into the throat, and back out of the forehead. Do this series of meditations as often as you like. But always do the Circle of Fire first. The Milky Way is to be used for creative purposes only. It is given to you, so that you can become more creative in all of your affairs. This is a meditation to prepare your body for the Nu-Ray, (Ring and Circle of Fire only).

Ring of Fire

For prosperity and good health, recite this affirmation daily (before or after the Milky Way meditation).

I am the rich radiant substance of the universe. I am the master of this substance. I take control of substance in my thoughts, words, and actions now.

Since divine substance is involved in all things, it is the one and only reality in all of my affairs and creations now. Now visualize it and it will be yours.

What I hope to convey to you is this. If you have not discovered the genius that you are, then you have not discovered your own self. That divine spark of Cosmic Man, which is a bright flame inside of him, is also in you. Every time you are inspired, you are touched with a small amount of this flame, or light. The greatest thing that can happen to you is to discover yourself. When you discover yourself, you discover your spirit. When you discover your spirit, you discover your higher self, your true nature. You will be aware of the unlimited power and knowledge, which you already have.

Listen for that still small voice, and when you hear it, believe it. It is easy to doubt yourself. The best way to know when you have heard that still small voice within is that you will be accompanied with inspiration. You will feel high. This still small voice is the voice of your spirit. Your higher self is your own spirit; your lower self is your ego, your body mind, your logical self. Both are needed in this world;

however, most are only in tune with their lower self. This occurs when you are only in tune with the material and the physical, your pleasurable desires. The moment you begin to listen to your inner-self, your spirit, you will become free of the body's desires. Body desires bring havoc and pain. Now, once you attain this high place within, you will become aware of the Universal One, the One we call God. Also, when you are in tune with your higher self, your body will work for you, not you being a slave for your body. If you can but attain just a spark of the Inner Spirit, you will feel inspiration.

Great spiritual beings from the past ages were always dwelling within the light, this same light of inspiration that I have been talking about. Once you achieve this, then you no longer have to sit in meditation; you will walk in it. You will breathe it. You will be it. The Light is life and the Light is love. No one can experience love unless he or she experiences the Light of Knowing, the Light of Inspiration.

If you have experienced this light then you must keep on seeking it. Because you can be swayed by your senses, until you have an illumination naturally, you will always have the desire for more light. Yet, just as I have swayed from it, you can also be drawn away from it. Now, I am back on track, back seeking more light, more love, more inspiration. My sole desire is to share this light within, and that I may experience more. This should be your only true desire also. Seek the quiet shores of the beaches where there are no crowds.

Seek the forests, for there the quiet natural sounds will speak to you. When you go by a small lake, or stream, sit quietly, listen to the sounds of nature. Then listen to your own breathing. Wait and listen for that still small voice within and you will hear it. I prefer to go outside in the middle of the evening. Seek always to be alone. There are plenty of times when you will be with loved ones. Take a long, quiet journey inside of yourself and you will find true beauty, true love.

Shun loud noises, loud and aggressive people, for they are destructive to your spirit, your soul. Have you noticed how mankind is seeking more thrills, more amusement parks, more aggressive movies? These surely are negative to your spirit. Your spirit is gentle, calm, and all loving. Why do we hurt it so, with loud noises, crowds, drugs, alcohol, and bright lights. Watch our children reaching out for loud and aggressive music. The louder the better is their motto. How can we teach our own children when we do not know any better?

It is not too late; it is never too late. Seek out gentle waterfalls, rainbows, flowers, and especially trees. As the Lakota Indians say, talk to the whales, wolves, and insects. The Spider Nation has much to say to you about how to live in harmony with nature. If you can live in harmony with nature, you can live in harmony with yourself. You can live in harmony with other humans. Until this happens, however, you will be lost in the world of illusion. The gentle rhythms of nature are in tune with your own heartbeat. We are standing at the dawn of the Golden Age. We are in the gateway of a new age of Light. If we do not enter now, we could slip back into another hundred years of darkness and destruction, of world domination of people, wars, murder, and rape.

I believe in my fellow man. I believe that it is never too late. We can at the last breath endure and enter this Golden Age. This Golden Age will bring magic, wisdom, and music such as you never heard. Your minds will open up to the golden light of magic and you will become masters of your own destiny. Happiness will prevail everywhere. It is up to each and every one of us to seek the Light, to aid our fellow man. Remember what the Master said, "Forgive them, Father, for they know not what they do," and "Seek first the Kingdom of Heaven, and all else will be given to you." The Kingdom is within you, not outside of you.

Man has created this monster, the devil. Actually, the word devil is slang. It comes from saying "do-evil" and the "o" was dropped and now it is devil. The word Satan is Greek and means adversary. Who is your adversary? None other than your own self. Man places the evil, the negative outside of you, and I say that everything is within, both the good and the evil. Which do you choose? It is that simple. When the Christ wrestled with the Devil, he wrestled with none other than his own self. He overcame and so shall we. He told us so. Listen to the truth and you will be-set free. Free from your negative self and free to be with your higher self, your true self. Wake up dear world and seek within where all truth lies.

No one has power over you, unless you give a person the power. "The things that I do, you can also do, saith the Lord." No one can conquer you, unless you allow it. I am not telling you to resist because resistance gives power. I am telling you to seek the gentle spirit that you are and you will become the KING. This is the reason why Jesus did not fight his enemies. Instead, he chose to go within. None of those who wanted to harm him could until he let them. Again, I say, you may have all of God's knowing if you become fully illuminated with the Great White Light, or you can get the Light in smaller doses and gradually become aware of his knowing. I believe that this is the best approach.

Think of this. If you were locked in a closet for eons of time and someone opened the door, your eyes would be burned out of your head. Instead, the door should be opened a crack at a time so that you could be adjusted to the light. Do not be dismayed if the Light comes in small doses; you will still get there. You always get whatever you desire the instant you desire it, but you must desire it with your soul, rather than through your senses. Many people will pray for something and never get it. That is because they ask with their body mind, rather than their spirit mind.

All prayers will be answered if asked with the soul rather than the senses. Praying with the body mind is nothing more than begging. Praying with your spirit means it will automatically be yours.

If you are in tune with the Universal One, your desires will come to you in the Language of Light. He talks to you in rhythms, in flashes of light. Then whatever you ask for within your heart, think it into the form of a concept by imagining it into a form. In other words, you visualize it inside of your mind into a form. You have to see it clearly in your mind in order for it to materialize in this physical universe. Do not put this form into action while it is still nebulous. Rather, place it in the back of your mind and go about your daily affairs and it will materialize. Later on, concentrate on it again and then let it fall in the back of your mind again. Do this everyday until you can picture it very clearly in your mind, as though it had already appeared.

Imagine it just the way you would if it were a baby inside of the womb. It has to slowly materialize in your mind, as a baby has to grow and materialize in the womb. You have to walk and talk it inside of your mind. Live it and breathe it until it materializes inside of your head.

Keep working on it daily, no matter what it is and it will surely be yours. Naturally, if it is an invention, it may take longer. You need to have patience and persistence. If you start experimenting on it before it is completely born inside of your head, then like a child that is born prematurely, it will not be completely physical. Hear it, see it, and feel it within your soul completely before you give it a body. Create it invisibly before you create it visibly. Always become absolutely still in a meditative state before you visibly act upon it.

Start off by breathing slowly and deeply. Then allow the pictured image of it to appear in your mind. See it as a completed product. Do this daily until you have it solely in your mind. Then you can act upon it and it will be done masterly. When you do act upon it, keep always in tune with your soul and then your soul with the Universal Soul. If you do this, you will notice that your work will be done swiftly and you will never tire while working on it. If you ever notice that your conscious mind or your ego is involved, stop immediately, otherwise you will become fatigued and your work will have flaws. Your physical emotions will always overpower your spiritual inspirations. When this happens, you will fail.

So be alert, and do not allow the emotions of your body to get involved. The moment you find yourself working alone with your conscious mind, stop working, for the emotions of your electric-sensed body are making you aware of it, and your work will be short-lived.
It is just like writing this book. I first was in tune with the Language of Light. Then I became inspired while in the Light of Inspiration. My desire was being fulfilled with the knowing, which the inspiration is. Now, the Language of Light is wordless, but in it is the essence of knowing; this knowing became my intelligence. Then I put my intelligence into words. This becomes my technique for writing.

All through this little book, you will feel my spirit and you will feel my ego. If I could have kept ego out of it completely, then this book would be a masterpiece. But, I am still on the path and receive my inspirations slowly and gradually. My only desire in this book is to inspire you to see the Light within yourself. With this in mind, I cannot fail. I can, however, make mistakes and I know that if you meditate before reading each chapter, you will find them and rectify them.

A masterpiece of any product whatsoever is that of the light of love of the Creator's soul, having been extended to it through your soul and re-extended to other souls through re-inspiration.

Here is an example: John Wesley had an inspiration. He then inspired others through his inspiration and thus the Methodist Church was born. However, as this inspiration was passed down, it began to lose some of its essence, and eventually the inspiration is lost, now all you have is dogma. This is what religion is. This is the meaning of religion.

# ABOUT THE AUTHOR

Born into a large family, Gordon Banta was raised in West Milford, (Greenwood Lake) New Jersey. He questioned strange childhood events and later became aware that his visions and gut feelings accurately predicted present and future situations. On several occasions his life was saved by these feelings. He thirsted for knowledge after reading nearly every book on metaphysics and psychic phenomenon. Banta sold his transportation business in 1974, moved to a small town (Deland, Fl) next to a small Spiritualist community "Cassadaga, Florida," and began devoting himself entirely to his spiritual and psychic development.

It took him two years to study to become a certified medium and later was ordained a "Spiritualist Minister." He also studied at the University of Science and Philosophy. His teachings get positive results! Gordon Banta is internationally known, having taught and helped people in all walks of life. He has done outstanding work in drug rehabilitation centers and prisons. His record for totally rehabilitating convicts in Florida is unsurpassed. He speaks before organizations and groups such as the V.F.W. and Rotary, Lions Club, Elks Lodges, and Masons Lodges. He has also spoken before groups at colleges; among them are Fairleigh Dickenson, Rutgers, Florida Tech, Florida University, Rollins College, and Colorado State.

Banta devotes his life to teaching and helping people to understand the mysteries and power of the inner mind. He says, "Psychic ability is innate and is an ability that everyone can develop." He teaches us that the right side of the brain is the intuitive side, or feminine side. Banta says, "Our subconscious mind knows everything; it is constantly receiving thoughts and is there for all of us to use."

Banta now resides in Swampscott, Massachusetts, and has joined the Spiritualist Church of Swampscott. He moved there from Orange City, Florida. For four years he was on a popular Radio Show (102 JHMS) in Orlando, called "Psychic Wednesdays with Psychic Gordon." He was a guest on the popular "Welch and Woody Show." Previously, Gordon Banta produced and hosted his own weekly (local origination) "The Gordon Banta Show," aired on TKR Channel 6 in Warren, New Jersey. He also produced, directed, and hosted the popular

"Vision Quest Show" on another channel in Nutley, New Jersey. Banta was featured in an Emmy-Winning production of "What's Happening America?" hosted by Shana Alexander and has repeatedly been asked to guest other national and local television talk shows, including the former "Joen Franklin Show," the longest running talk show on television to this date.

Banta's first published book *Creative Dreams* was published by the Mandala Press in 2005 and is distributed widely by Sun Rising Books.